BASS GUITAR
BEGINNERS
JUMPSTART

Learn Basic Lines, Rhythms and Play Your First Songs

ANDY SCHNEIDER

Listen to This Book!

Download the free audio examples of these exercises

Scan and go now

SEEINGMUSICBOOKS.COM

SEEING MUSIC
METHOD BOOKS

Introduction

I love learning. I love getting new skills that give me new abilities. And, I love passing on those skills to others so that they can enjoy their own talents and new abilities. This book is for the absolute beginner. Welcome.

It's always a good time to start learning music and the guitar. Students of any age can see real results from a good practice routine. Many, many adults and children have benefitted from my teaching method and I hope you'll soon have new abilities to make your own music.

In my years teaching guitar and talking with other professional string players, I've noticed that we all have developed an ability to "see" the music we play on the fretboard of the instrument. We see the music we play as a simple relationship of shapes and relative positions. Look at these two shapes:

Just as you recognize the shapes above, stringed instrumentalists see music on the fretboard of their instrument. This is an inherently special gift we who play stringed instruments have been given. No other kind of instrument makes it so easy for the musician to have a visual roadmap of the music, making things like improvisation or transposing a song to another key so easy. Our fingers follow these maps to get to the music. This book will show you how to see music as simple shapes and use these shapes to more quickly and proficiently play and create music.

We'll be covering how music is constructed and 'looks' on the neck of the guitar. While we won't get into any particular musical style or specific techniques, the information here is common to all Western music: Rock, Folk, Country, Pop, Classical, Jazz.

While the first steps of guitar playing are the same for everyone, the next few steps of learning chords can be taught many different ways. I'm going to walk you through what I believe is the fastest and most powerful way. Learning guitar chords with a visual method makes it so much easier and minimizes memorization. You will develop life-long skills that you will use every day you pick up a guitar.

Turn the page: you're about to "see" music!

SEEING MUSIC
METHOD BOOKS

CONTENTS

SELECTING YOUR FIRST BASS

Acoustic or Electric

Most bass guitars are electric and meant to be amplified with an amplifier. There are such things as acoustic bass guitars but they are usually not great for playing without an amplifier. Without an amp, the sound isn't very loud and has a rather thin tone. So whichever you choose, plan to buy an amplifier. Bass amps are specially designed to reproduce bass sounds and withstand the rather large output signal that bass guitars produce. Practice amps have smaller speakers and cost less than professional models which have larger or more powerful speakers. So, leave a little in your budget for an amp. There are many inexpensive practice amps that will work just fine.

Size and Playability

This bit is crucial. Guitars come in many sizes, often described by their scale length. *Scale* is literally the length of the string, measured from the bridge to the nut (see chapter *Know Your Guitar* for details). If you're a smaller person, you may want to look for shorter scale bass. Full size is 34" while medium and short scales are 32" and 30". Generally, 34" scale is considered to have the best tone, while shorter scales offer easier playability.

Another factor is the playability or *action* of the neck. Action refers to how easily the bass plays. For good action, the strings must be fairly close to the frets, but not so close they create a buzzing sound. If you're unfamiliar with how good action feels, ask someone with experience for their opinion of your bass guitar candidate. Since the action of most basses can be adjusted by a technician, if you already own a one, they may be able to improve its playability at your local repair shop.

Each time the bass is outfitted with different gauge strings, the action changes and the guitar will need a little adjustment. This operation is usually refered to as a *set-up* and involves adjusting the height of the strings, the bow of the neck (yes, necks are supposed to be slightly bowed) and sometimes adjusting the string slots in the nut.

Price

This is a big one, obviously. Some people like to be value-minded and find an inexpensive bass to begin their study. Some people like to make a big investment right away, buying a beautiful instrument from a well-reputed manufacturer. Perhaps it helps them stay motivated to learn or they view it as an investment. Either way, there are great basses for beginners at all prices. Generally, more expensive models have better tone and some high-quality features, such as more adjustability for the owner's playing style.

Strings

Most electric basses will come with metal, *roundwound* strings. These are great, all-purpose strings. Roundwound strings have a solid metal wire core and are wrapped with a smaller, round wire. If you look at the string closely, you'll see the bumps of the wound string. If you run your finger along the string, it feels scalloped, like the edge of a zipper. There are also *flatwound* strings which are also called *tapewound*. These have a smooth, round tone and are also a little easier on fingers. Additionally, flatwound strings also come with either a flat metal wrap or a flat nylon wrap which is often black. These nylon flatwounds have an even softer tone, very much approximating the sound of an upright bass. There are lots of choices and you'll have many opportunities to experiment.

Quality of Tuners

This is a bigger issue than you might think. Good quality tuners turn very smoothly and help keep the bass in tune. Poor ones make it difficult to tune or even cause the bass to slip out of tune. If you can, try their feel. If you're buying without being able to try them, know that the cost of the instrument is generally an indicator of the quality. Not always, but generally more expensive basses come with more high-quality tuners.

Pickups

Most every bass guitar comes with one or two pickups. While you'll be able to see magnetic pickups mounted under the strings on the body, acoustic/electric basses generally use a pickup located inside the bridge. Again, cost generally indicates the quality. More pickups means more tonal variety, but shouldn't affect your enjoyment of the guitar.

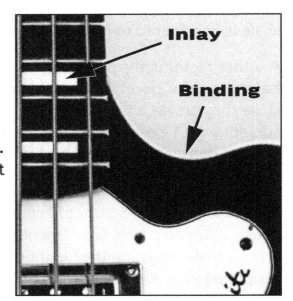

FIG.1 - INLAY AND BINDING

Other Fancy Stuff

There's lots of things that get added to basses to either dress them up or add functionality. Adornments like inlays and binding add visual appeal but not playability. Examples of functional upgrades include electronic tuners (indicating whether the instrument is in tune), active electronics (those with a pre-amplifier inside the guitar) or a carrying case. Yes it's strange, but most basses are sold without a case. Leave a little money in your budget for one of those, as well. Soft cases are called gig-bags and often come with backpack-style straps while hard shell cases offer the best protection.

BASS GUITAR CARE AND MAINTENANCE

Storage

Basses are a lot like people: They don't like things too hot or too cold, too wet or too dry. Avoid leaving your bass in very hot or cold places, like a car. A great rule of thumb is, if you would be uncomfortable with the temperature or humidity of a place, don't leave your instrument there.

When putting away your bass, a hard-shell case is the safest location. A guitar stand is also acceptable. Avoid leaning your bass against a wall or furniture. If it slips and falls over, it could easily be damaged or broken. Also, avoid leaving it near heaters, radiators or even in bright sunshine.

Cleaning

Keep your bass clean with guitar polish and a soft rag or polish cloth. Generally, a light spritz of polish and wiping with the polish cloth is all that's necessary. Your instrument's manufacturer may have special recommendations to follow.

Replacing Strings

Strings wear out over time and with use. If you see any discoloration, like rust, or evidence of wear, like dents where the strings meet the frets, buy a new set of strings and have them replaced by a technician. If you're replacing strings yourself, be aware that they can spring up and poke your eyes. Consider wearing safety eyewear. Seriously. Your eyes deserve protection.

FIG.2 - BASS ON GUITAR STAND

DAY 1 - PROPER PLAYING POSITION

LAY A GREAT FOUNDATION

Great music begins with correct posture and instrument position. Start from a sitting position in a chair that allows your upper legs to be parallel to the ground. Hold the bass close to your body, with the neck pointing slightly upward so your left hand is approximately level with your right elbow. If the neck sags too low to the floor, you'll have to reach farther with your left hand and playing will be difficult and uncomfortable. To aid this, you may want to raise your right heel so the body of the bass rises up about an inch. Let your heel rest on your chair leg.

FIG.3 - PROPER INSTRUMENT POSITION

FIG.4 - GOOD HAND POSITION

Notice in the pictures how the left thumb is directly behind the neck and the wrist is straight. A straight wrist is essential for good technique, but also the hardest part for many students to achieve. In the next chapter, we'll see why.

FIG.5 - RAISED HEEL UNDER BASS BODY

Whatever you do, don't worry about trying to look cool. Lots of pro rock stars are known for wearing their bass really low, or slouching, or even jumping in the air. While you're learning the fundamentals, the more time you spend focused on correct posture and technique, the faster you'll get where you want to go. In fact, refer to this chapter often. Remember to always check your alignment and return to good hand and body position if they slip.

The bass is tuned, low to high, E, A, D and G. If you're experienced you can tune by ear, but the easiest way to tune is to buy an electronic guitar/bass tuner. Many are available inexpensively. Alternatively, there are lots of great tuners available for phones and tablets. Many of these apps are free, so if you have a smart device, check its app store.

The strings of the bass are numbered from the highest pitch to the lowest. The highest and lightest string is the first string and the lowest and heaviest string is the fourth string.

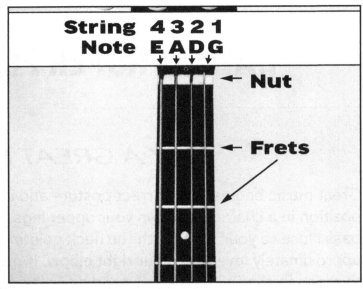

FIG.6 - STRING NOTE NAMES

A NOTE ABOUT FINGERNAILS

Long fingernails and guitar playing don't really go well together. If you've got long nails on your fretting hand, you'll find they get in the way of good finger position. They also tend to dig in the wood of the fretboard. Long nails on the picking hand tend to get scuffed or interfere with fingerstyle picking. While long nails may look pretty, you may have to make a tough choice to cut them.

FRETBOARD DIAGRAMS

HOW TO READ FRETBOARD DIAGRAMS

You're ready to start learning some notes. The diagrams in this book are kind of like pictures of what you'll see when you look at your bass.

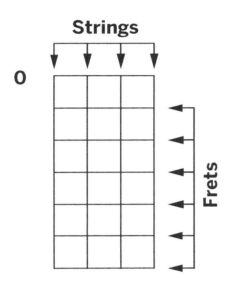

FIG.7 - FRET NOTATION

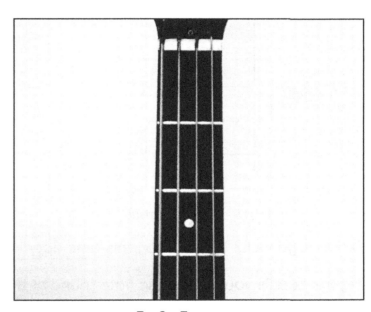

FIG.8 - FRETBOARD

Hold your bass upright in front of you and look at fretboard. The strings run up and down, the frets run horizontally. That is the view used in fretboard diagrams.

The names of the open-strings in order from lowest pitch to highest are E, A, D and G. While it seems logical to conceive of music from the lowest pitches to the highest, the numbering of the strings goes against this concept. The strings of the bass are numbered from the highest to the lowest. So, open G is the 1st string and open E is the 4th string.

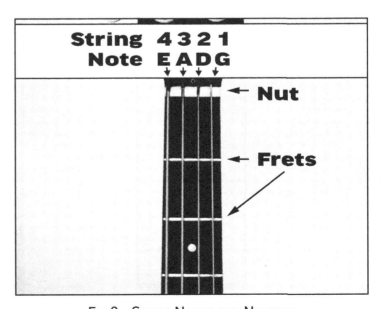

FIG.9 - STRING NAMES AND NUMBERS

Try playing your first note. As indicated in Figure 10, play open E, the 4th string. An open circle indicates an open string, one that is played without fretting with the left hand.

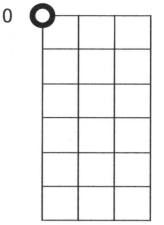

FIG.10 - OPEN 6TH STRING

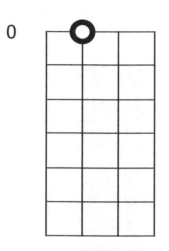

FIG.11 - OPEN 5TH STRING

With your picking hand, feel free to use a pick or just your fingers. For now, do whatever is comfortable.

Did that go well? Try another, this time open A, the 3rd string.

Figure 12 tells you to play the note found at the black dot on the 3rd String at the 3rd fret. It's the 3rd fret because it's three frets higher up the neck than the "0" in the upper-left corner of the diagram. The zero indicates that the diagram begins at the nut or "zeroth" fret.

The "2" next to the black dot indicates you'll use your 2nd finger of your fretting hand as in Figure 13.

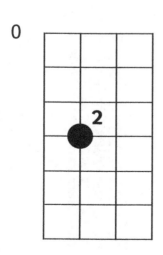

FIG.12 - FRET NOTATION

FIG.13 - LEFT-HAND FINGERING

14 BASS GUITAR BEGINNERS JUMPSTART: A SEEING MUSIC METHOD BOOK

On these diagrams, a filled-in circle indicates that you'll put your finger at that fret. Actually, you'll put your finger just behind the fret, not right on top of the fret. The fret, not your finger, is what stops the vibration of the string and changes it's length.

Keeping your finger pressed with medium pressure, just behind the fret will produce the clearest and best sound.

Don't confuse a fretboard diagram with a musical staff. Music staves indicate pitch and rhythm. Fretboard diagrams like Figure 12 are like a roadmap, showing you where to place your fingers.

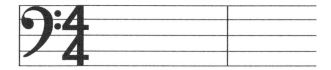

FIG.14 - MUSICAL STAFF

A NOTE ABOUT FRETBOARD DIAGRAMS

Most other books place the dot in-between the fret lines. While they're trying to be helpful, this just confuses the learning process. When you see a dot in this book, you'll know that it is showing you the note to be played and that you'll place your finger just behind that fret to hear it.

SOUNDCHECK

Fretboard diagrams indicate where to find a note and what finger to use to play it.

The number in the upper-left corner of a fretboard diagram indicates on which fret the diagram begins.

Fretboard diagrams should not be confused with musical staves.

DAY 2 - PLAYING SINGLE NOTES

||||||||||||||||||||||||||||||||||||||||||||||||||||||||||||||||||||||||||||||||||

MILESTONE

As you pass each milestone, take a moment to recall previous lessons.

Have a seat with your bass in good playing position.

||||||||||||||||||||||||||||||||||||||||||||||||||||||||||||||||||||||||||||||||||

Ready to start making music? Let's start with some open string notes.

You'll remember these notes from yesterday's lesson about the names of the strings.

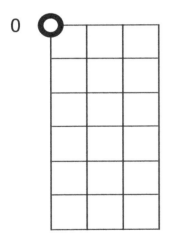

FIG.15 - OPEN 6TH STRING (E)

Start by playing open E. Using either your right-hand fingers or a pick, sound open E on the 6th string. This is the lowest note on the bass and maybe the most fun to play!

Now try open A. Feel free to look down at your right hand so you cleanly sound just the 3rd string. It's easy to hit other strings in the process, so keep focused on just hitting the A string.

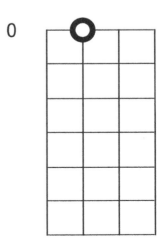

FIG.16 - OPEN 5TH STRING (A)

GOOD FRETTING TECHNIQUE

You've also already played C on the 3rd string. Give it a try, using your fretting hand 2nd finger.

Remember, your fret finger will go just behind the fret (slightly toward the nut).

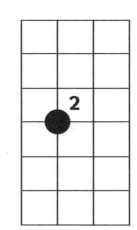

FIG.17 - 3RD STRING C

On the 4th string, the 3rd fret is G. Use the 2nd finger of your fretting hand on the 3rd fret, as well.

Now repeat, playing C on the 3rd string, then G on the 4th. Do this a few more times.

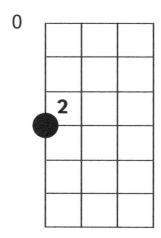

FIG.18 - 4TH STRING G

SOUNDCHECK

Now, how do things sound? Are you getting any buzzes? Is the note full and ringing? Most students need several days of this exercise before the notes sound clean and pleasant. If you're having trouble, make certain that your fretting finger is very near the fret. This is crucial. In fact, you'll be so close that you're almost on top of the fret. When you get the feel of it, it will make everything else easier. Keep trying!

Also, keep your wrist straight, not bent. Remember that tilting the neck up and keeping the fretboard near your shoulder will make this easier. Playing guitar should never be uncomfortable, so if your fingers, hands, arms or anywhere else starts to hurt, stop right away. Sometimes fingertips get sore after a practice session, especially if a player is just starting out. In time, callouses develop, making playing less uncomfortable.

PUTTING IT ALL TOGETHER

Every note has a beginning and an end, right? While there's only one way to pick a string, there are two ways to stop it. Let's put it all together, starting and stopping each of the four notes.

Play open A, then open E. Start each note with your pick or thumb, then stop each note by lightly touching the strings with your left fingers. Try it again, picking the note with your right hand, then "catching" the strings with your left to stop the note.

Similarly, pick C then G. These are fretted notes, so if you let up the pressure with your fretting hand, the note will stop ringing.

Give it a try. Pluck with your right, then semi-release the pressure with your left hand just to the point the note stops ringing.

FIG.19 - LEFT HAND MUTING

Tinker with the speed and pressure change with your fretting hand until the note stops cleanly.

Ok, now let's stop these notes a different way. This time, you'll use your picking hand to stop the note. This is called palm muting and it's like putting the brakes on a car.

If you're using a pick, you'll use the bottom of your picking hand, the soft bottom edge of your hand that's between your pinky and wrist. Pick a note, then use your palm's edge to stop it. Is the note stopping cleanly?

FIG.20 - PICKING POSITION

FIG.21 - PALM MUTING

FIG.22 - RIGHT HAND MUTING E STRING

If you're using your fingers to pluck the note, simply pluck the string and then bring that finger back to rest on the same string. See how fast you can go from picking the note to stopping it. See how slowly you can do the same. Pretty neat, huh?

ABOUT STAFF NOTATION

Music staffs are a great, efficient way to describe rhythm. Here is a staff indicating Bass Clef and time signature. Bass Clef means it's describing lower notes (not treble notes) and the time signature tells us how to count. Most, but not all, music is in 4, meaning we count one measure "1, 2, 3, 4." The top number 4 is that number. The bottom number means that what we are counting is quarter notes. Just as with apples or dollars, a quarter is 1/2 of a half. A half is 1/2 of a whole.

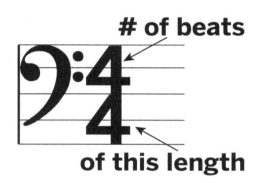

FIG.23 - 4/4 TIME SIGNATURE

So, our staff here indicates we are in the Treble Clef. The song is in 4/4 time, which means there are 4 beats of quarter notes in each measure. A measure is indicated by the vertical lines on the staff.

FIG.24 - QUARTER-NOTE REST

Figure 24 shows a quarter-note rest. Where notes (or in this book, hash marks) tell us when to play, rests tell us when not to play. Take a little rest!

Today's Assignment

Let's practice starting and stopping notes cleanly. The hash marks on the staff tell you when to play a note, the name of the note is above it. The rests tell you when to mute the strings for silence.

Rhythm Tip: Slowly say "One, Two, Three, Four". Now, say the same thing, but whisper on "Two" and "Four".

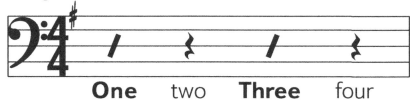

FIG.25 - COUNTING QUARTER-NOTES AND RESTS

It should sound like "ONE, two, THREE, four". Now, imitate that with your bass, "ONE, two, THREE, four". Keep repeating this exercise, slowly at first.

FIG.26 - E AND A

FIG.27 - G AND C

FIG.28 - G AND C ALTERNATING

FIG.29 - C, G, E AND A

22 BASS GUITAR BEGINNERS JUMPSTART: A SEEING MUSIC METHOD BOOK

DAY 3 - THE MAJOR SCALE

||||||||||||||||||||||||||||||||||||||||||||||||||||||||||||||||||||||||||

MILESTONE

At the 3rd fret, play C on the 3rd string and G on the 4th string.

Remember: Your fretting finger should be just behind the fret; the closer, the better.

||||||||||||||||||||||||||||||||||||||||||||||||||||||||||||||||||||||||||

THE AWESOME POWER OF SCALES

Scales are awesome because ALL music comes from them! Melodies come from scales. Chords come from scales and so do bass lines. And scales are easy to memorize, which will make learning bass lines easy, too.

Take a look at the C Major scale. The notes of the C Major scale in order are C, D, E, F, G, A, B and C.

CDEFGABC

FIG.30 - C MAJOR SCALE NOTE NAMES

All the notes here are separated by a whole-step, except those indicated by the "^" symbol. Those are separated by a half-step. On the bass, two notes that are one fret apart are separated by a half-step. Two half-steps equals one whole step, which would be two frets distance.

Again, most notes here are one whole-step apart, with the exception being those separated by a half-step.

HOW TO PLAY A MAJOR SCALE

In Figure 31, start on the 3rd string, 3rd fret and place your 2nd finger there. It's indicated by the dot with the "X" through it. This is the root, C.

Play the C, then keeping your 2nd finger there, add your 4th finger at the 5th fret on the same string. Play this note, D.

Now, you can release these notes. On the 2nd string at the 2nd fret, place your 1st finger. Play this E.

Next play F, then G, then on to the 1st string, similarly. At the end, you'll reach the high C.

The finger you should use for each fret is indicated in Figure 31.

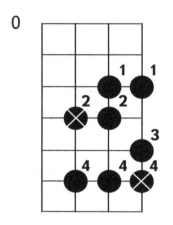

FIG.31 - C MAJOR SCALE

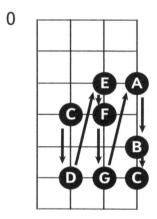

FIG.32 - C MAJOR SCALE
NOTE NAMES

MORE ABOUT MAJOR SCALES

A major scale is a series of whole and half-steps.

A half-step is the distance between two notes that are one fret apart. A whole-step is equal to two half-steps.

In all major scales, the half-steps are between the 3rd and 4th notes (or *degrees*) and the 7th and root degrees. All the other notes are a whole step apart, or the equivalent of two frets in distance from each other.

In the C Major scale, the half-steps are between E and F and between B and C. Take note of them in Figure 32.

To easily remember the fingering of the C Major scale, use this tip:

On the A-string, you use fingers 2 and 4. Next, on the D-string, you use fingers 1, 2 and 4 and on the G-string, you use 1, 3 and 4.

When you say it to yourself a few times, it even starts to sound kind of musical. Say, "2 4, 1 2 4, 1 3 4."

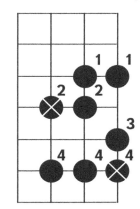

FIG.33 - C MAJOR SCALE

Today's Assignment

Sure, scales help your fingers get used to finding their way around the neck, but aren't they a little boring? No! They will be your superpower, soon letting you access any bass line, any melody, anytime.

Play C Major starting with the lowest note (C on the 3rd string) and ending with the highest note (C on the 1st string). Play this a few times until you can make the string changes easily and smoothly.

If you find it difficult to reach all the notes, stop and examine your wrist. Is it bent? It shouldn't be. When your wrist is straight, you'll have the greatest reach possible. Make some adjustments to the angle of your guitar, your wrist, arm and possibly even your guitar height. Review the chapter "Proper Playing Position".

After you successfully can play all 8 notes going up the scale, play them in reverse order, descending down the scale. Start with the top note, C on the 1st string, and work your way down to C on the 3rd string.

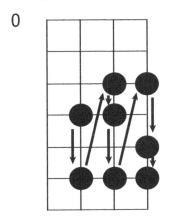

FIG.34 - C MAJOR ASCENDING

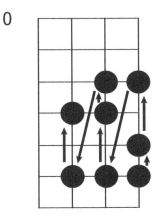

FIG.35 - C MAJOR DESCENDING

QUARTER, HALF AND WHOLE NOTES

As you probably know, a measure of 4 beats is common in Western music. These are generally quarter notes. And just like the coins that may be in your pocket right now, two quarters are the same as a half and two halfs are the same as a whole.

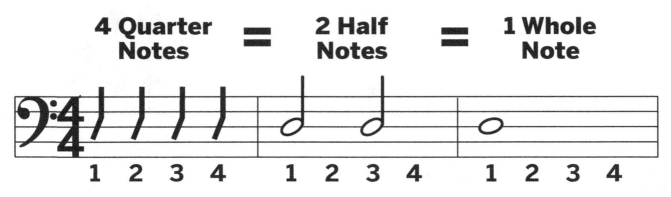

FIG.36 - NOTE LENGTH EQUIVALENTS

Examine the quarter, half and whole notes above. The type of note (quarter, half or whole) tells the musician how long to hold the note. Measures are composed of these combinations of note values and those note values always total 4 in any measure of 4/4 time.

Playing Whole Notes

Before playing on your bass, start by just counting measures of four. Slowly say outloud, "One, Two, Three, Four". With steady timing, repeat this counting several times. The time in-between "Four" and the next measure's "One" should be the same as the time in-between any other two counts.

One   Two   Three   Four

FIG.37 - COUNTING TO FOUR

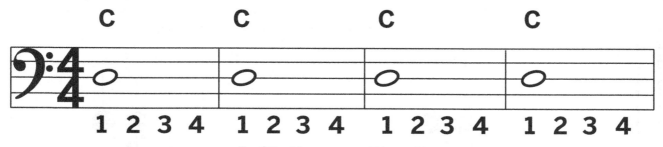

FIG.38 - MEASURES OF WHOLE NOTES

Now, play a whole note C on the downbeat (the "One" count) of each measure. Each time you say "One", play the note C and let it ring while continuing to count to "Four". Repeat several times.

Whole notes last for four counts. Does this match what you're playing?

Here's where things get exciting! This time, instead of repeating the same note, each time you say "One", advance to the next note in the C Major scale. Start with C for a four-count, then D for a four-count, then E and so on until you reach the high C at the end of the scale.

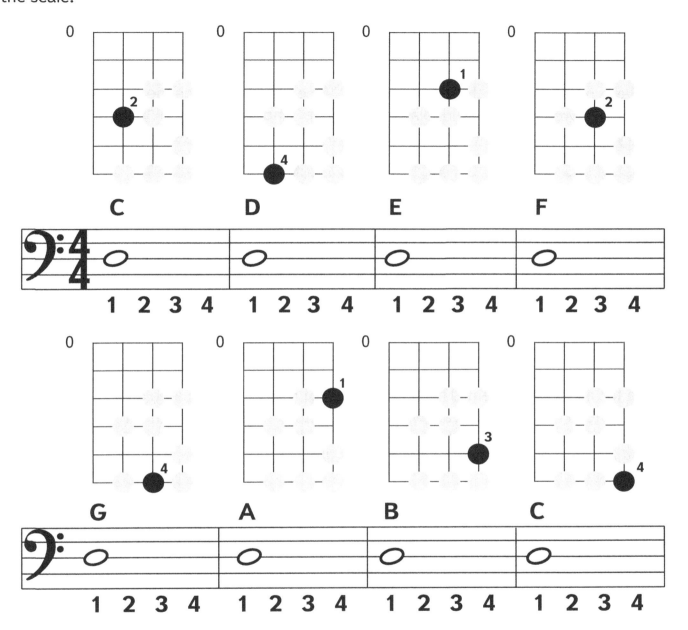

FIG.39 - CLIMBING WHOLE NOTES

A Note About These Music Staffs

Ordinarily, musical staffs are used to indicate which note is to be played as well as its duration. This is not the case in this book.

The staff indications here are just for rhythm and each note is simply indicating <u>when</u> to play a note, not <u>which</u> note to play. If you're experienced at reading music from staff paper, don't be confused! All the notes are a kind of hash mark, drawn on the middle line of the staff. They are not intended to tell you which note to play.

Playing Half Notes

Just as before, start by just counting measures of four. Slowly say outloud, "One, Two, Three, Four" but this time, put a little emphasis on "One" and "Three". It should sound like "ONE, two, THREE, four".

One two **Three** four

FIG.40 - COUNTING WITH EMPHASIS ON "ONE" AND "THREE"

Now, play a half note C on the downbeat (the "One" count) of each measure and hold it through the "Two" count. Again, play C on "Three" and hold through "Four. It will sound like every time you say "One" or "Three", you'll pick the note C. Repeat several times.

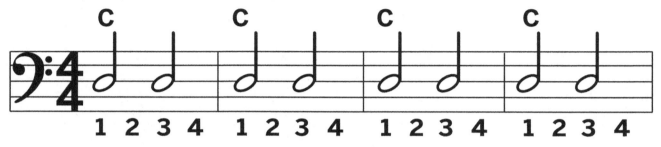

FIG.41 - MEASURES OF HALF NOTES

Half notes last for two counts. Does this match what you're playing?

Prepare for more excitement! This time, instead of repeating the same note, advance to the next note in the C Major scale with each half note. You'll start with C ("One, Two" and then D ("Three, Four") and then E ("One, Two") and then F ("Three, Four") and so on until you reach the high C at the end of the scale.

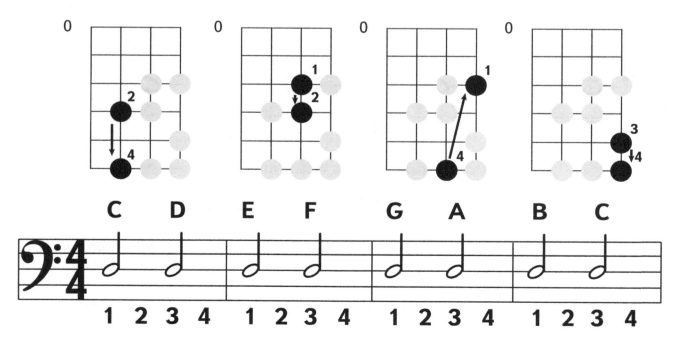

FIG.42 - MEASURES OF CLIMBING HALF NOTES

Playing Quarter Notes

Now, play quarter note C on each beat of the measure. With every count, "One, Two, Three, Four", play C. It will sound like every time you count from one to four, you'll have played four C notes. Repeat several times.

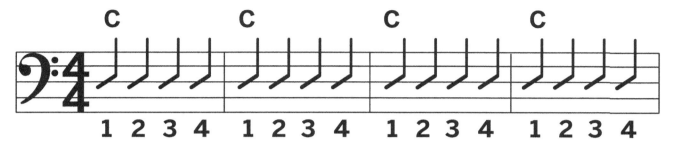

FIG.43 - MEASURES OF QUARTER NOTES

Quarter notes last for only one count each. Does this match what you're playing?

This time, instead of repeating the same note, advance to the next note in the C Major scale with each quarter note. You'll start with C on "One", then D on "Two" and then E on "Three" and so on until you reach the high C at the end of the scale. Then, start at the high-C and descend back down: C, B, A, G, F, E, D, C.

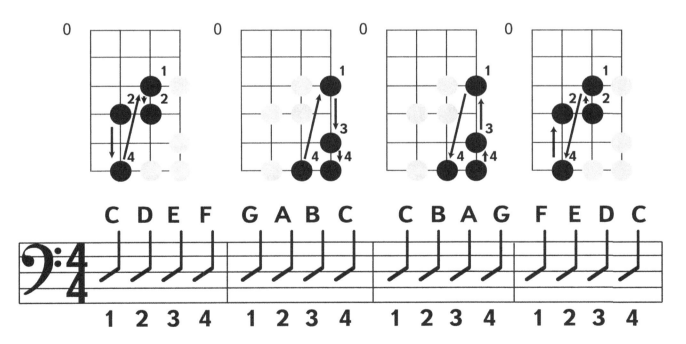

FIG.44 - MEASURES OF CLIMBING QUARTER NOTES

If any of these exercises are difficult, repeat perhaps a little more slowly until you can make it all the way to the end of the scale smoothly.

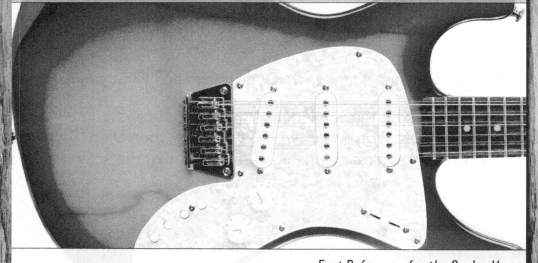

30 BASS GUITAR BEGINNERS JUMPSTART: A SEEING MUSIC METHOD BOOK

KNOW YOUR FRETBOARD (PART I)

||||||||||||||||||||||||||||||||||||||||||||||||||||||||||||||||||||||||||

One of the most important steps to playing bass is learning the names of the notes on the fretboard. If you know every note, everything else will be much easier to learn and play. And while the fretboard seems like a huge mess to be memorized, there are some super-easy shortcuts that will make learning much more fun.

||||||||||||||||||||||||||||||||||||||||||||||||||||||||||||||||||||||||||

THE FIRST 3 FRETS

Let's consider just the natural notes, those without sharps or flats. Start by playing all of the notes here, one at a time, starting at the bottom.

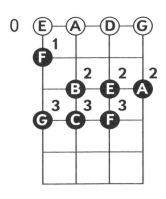

FIG.45 - FIRST 3 FRET
NOTE NAMES

Begin with the open 4th string, noted in the upper-left corner of the diagram. Say the note's name, E, as you play the note.

Next, put your 1st finger at 1st fret of that string, F, and say its name. Then use your 3rd finger to play the 3rd fret, again saying its name, G.

Next, move to the open A string. Keep going, playing B and C, then moving to the 2nd string. Keep ascending that way, moving up the fretboard and across the strings until you get all the way to the high-A at the far right of the figure.

The pitch you hear should get progressively higher with each note.

Note: These notes don't always have to be played with the fingering given here. This is just a good way to begin playing through all the notes.

MEMORIZING THESE EASILY

Memorizing things can be frustrating. Here's an easy way to remember the locations of the notes in Figure 45.

There really are only three fingerings to remember here. Notice that two strings share similar fingerings.

First, notice how the 3rd and 2nd strings — A and D — use the same pattern: open string, 2nd fret and 3rd fret.

Second, notice how the 4th string uses a slightly different pattern of open string, 1st fret and 3rd fret?

The 1st string, G, is easy to remember because there's only one fretted note to remember, 2nd fret.

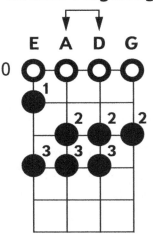

Similar Fingerings

Fig.46 - First 3 Fret Fingerings

SEEING MUSIC

Do you see how the notes of the A and D strings can be played with similar fingerings?

Do you see how the fingering of the E string is almost, but not exactly the same as the 2nd and 3rd strings?

Today's Assignment

Play all the natural notes from the exercise above in ascending order, saying the note names as you go.

Once you get those memorized, challenge yourself by playing them in descending order.

DAY 4 - C AND G MAJOR

||||||||||||||||||||||||||||||||||||||||||||||||||||||||||||||||||||||||||||||

MILESTONE

Play the C Major scale from earlier.

Scales types (like the major scale) are defined by their combination of whole and half-steps and the note they start on (the root).

Let's start a major scale on a different note, G.

||||||||||||||||||||||||||||||||||||||||||||||||||||||||||||||||||||||||||||||

HOW TO PLAY A G MAJOR SCALE

Below are the scales for C Major and G Major. Notice how they look very similar? That's because they both use the same combination of whole and half-steps. That's not surprising because ALL major scales use the same combination of whole and half-steps.

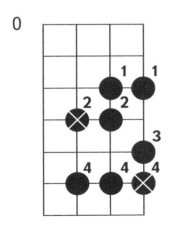

Fig.47 - C Major Scale

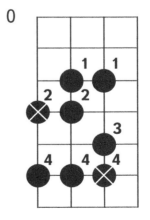

Fig.48 - G Major Scale

Just as you did with C Major, start with your 2nd finger. This time place it on the 4th string at the 3rd fret. Follow the diagram, playing the ascending scale.

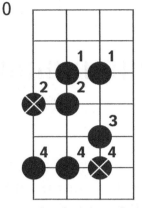

FIG.49 - G MAJOR SCALE

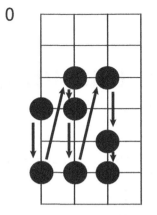

FIG.50 - G MAJOR SCALE

Here are the note names of the scale you just played.

FIG.51 - G MAJOR NOTE NAMES

See how the half-steps are between the 3rd and 4th, 7th and root degrees of the scale? This is just the same in the C Major scale and every other major scale.

See the symbol by F, the 7th degree? That is a sharp symbol. That means that it is one half-step higher than F natural.

ALL ABOUT SHARPS AND FLATS

When a note is raised a half-step, we say it is *sharp*. When a note is lowered a half-step, we say it is *flat*. When it is neither, we say it is *natural*.

Here are three notes, C, C# and D. Because C sharp is also one half-step below D, we could also call it by another name: D flat. D flat and C sharp are the same note.

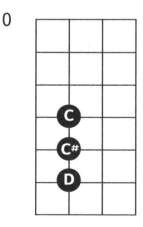

FIG.52 - C, C# AND D

Similarly, here are F, F# and G. We could call the middle note either F sharp or G flat.

It's OK to describe a note by its natural name, such as *F natural* and *G natural*. However, for the sake of convenience, musicians generally just say "F" and "G".

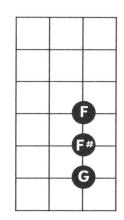

FIG.53 - F, F# AND D

PLAYING PENTATONIC SCALES

There are many types of scales in the musical universe. You've already seen one type of scale: the major scale. Another type is called the *pentatonic* scale. It's called pentatonic because it is made of 5 notes. Just as the name implies, it has 5 tones.

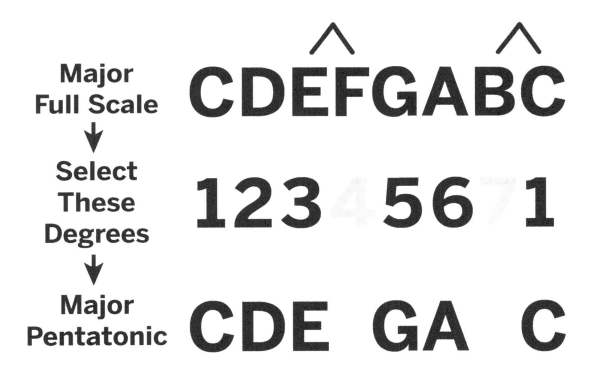

FIG.54 - MAJOR SCALE BECOMING PENTATONIC SCALE

In the figure above you can see that certain notes from the C Major scale were selected to create the C Major Pentatonic scale. Major pentatonics always include the root, 2nd, 3rd, 5th and 6th degrees. It's a very clever subset of the major scale that sounds great played on the bass, as you're about to hear.

Follow the diagram on the right, starting with the scale root, C. Use the fingering in the diagram, starting with your 2nd finger.

How did it go? Believe it or not, you just played your first bass part. Give yourself a big ol' 5-fingered pat on the back!

The major pentatonic scale gets used very frequently by bass players in all forms of popular music. It's worth getting to know.

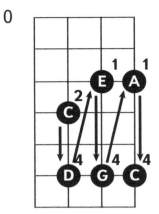

FIG.55 - C MAJOR PENTATONIC

Major Full Scale → **Select These Degrees** → **Major Pentatonic**

FIG.56 - MAJOR SCALE BECOMING PENTATONIC SCALE

Now have a look at the G Major Pentatonic which, as you already know, is a subset of the G Major scale.

Play this scale starting from the 4th string, 3rd fret with your 2nd finger. Play the G Major Pentatonic, then the C Major Pentatonic and back to the G Major Pentatonic. Repeat this a few times.

Can you hear a similarity between the scales? Do you see how these two scales share a similar shape? This is what is meant by "Seeing Music"!

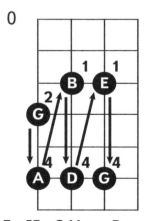

FIG.57 - G MAJOR PENTATONIC

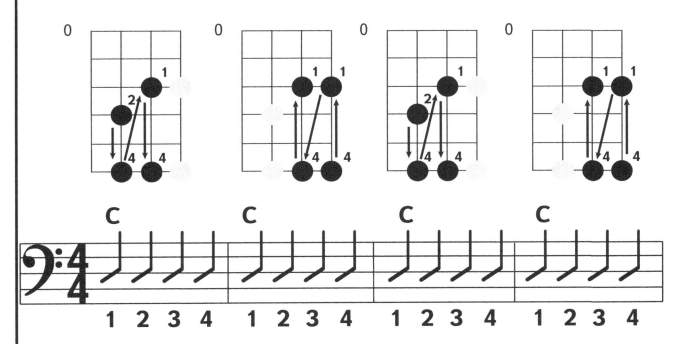

Look for the similarity between the G and C Major scales in Figures 47 and 48. Now notice the similarity between the G and C Major Pentatonics in Figures 55 and 57. This visual similarity is reflected in their sound similarity. Using the visual look of a scale makes it easier to remember and even move to a different place on the bass neck to become a new, but similar scale.

Today's Assignment

Here are a couple chord progressions using G and C Pentatonic scales.

In these charts, play the notes in the fretboard diagram in the order they are indicated, one note for each hash mark. Notice how some patterns are ascending, others are descending.

The chord symbol is above each measure. You'll be playing notes from that pentatonic scale. Take notice of it because sometimes it changes, so you'll have to change the scale you're using, too.

FIG.58 - C MAJOR PENTATONIC BASS LINE

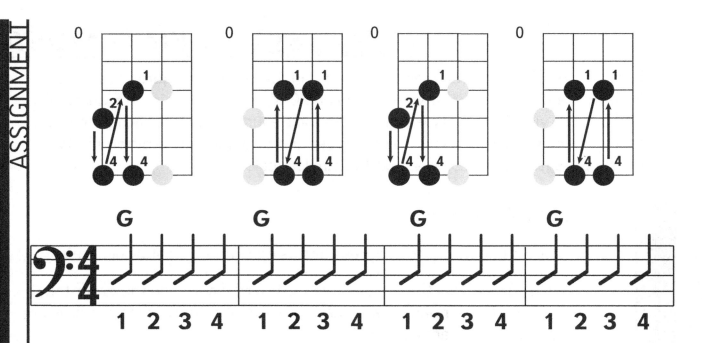

Fig.59 - G Major Pentatonic Bass Line

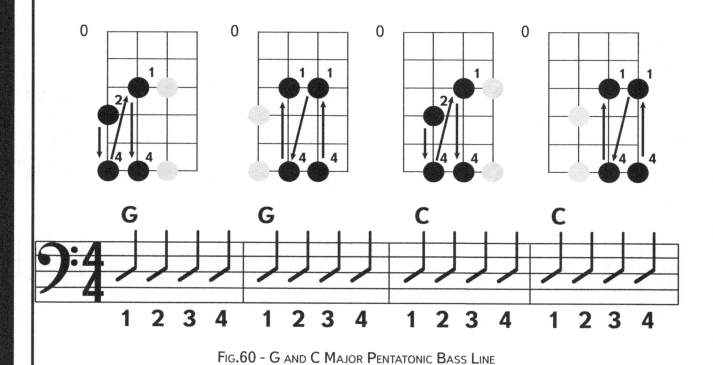

Fig.60 - G and C Major Pentatonic Bass Line

DAY 5 - A AND E MAJOR

||||||||||||||||||||||||||||||||||||||||||||||||||||||||||||||||||||||||||

MILESTONE

Play the C Major and G Major Pentatonic scales from yesterday. Remember how they use the same pattern, or shape?

Here you saw that a scale pattern can be moved back and forth across the fretboard to create a new scale. Now you'll see that they also can be moved *up and down* to create new scales.

||||||||||||||||||||||||||||||||||||||||||||||||||||||||||||||||||||||||||

A MAJOR PENTATONIC

Examine the G Major Pentatonic on the left. On the right is an A Major Pentatonic. It's in the key of A Major because it starts on A.

Play the G Major Pentatonic which starts on the 3rd fret, then play the A Major Pentatonic starting on the 5th fret. Notice how the number in the upper left of the diagram has changed from 0 to 4. Remember that this number indicates the fret on which the diagrams start.

Since the first note of the A Major Pentatonic is one fret higher than 4, it must be on the 5th fret.

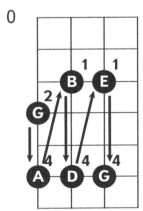

FIG.61 - G MAJOR PENTATONIC

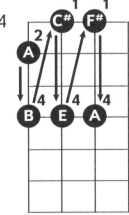

FIG.62 - A MAJOR PENTATONIC

Notice both scales use the same finger pattern and have the same shape. Their only difference is that they begin on different notes.

Now you know three Major Pentatonic scales: C, G and A. They all use the same shape. Now have a look at the A Major Pentatonic played using a different fingering.

A NEW PENTATONIC PATTERN

One of the great things about the bass guitar is that many notes can be played on different strings, at different places on the fretboard.

You just played the A Major Pentatonic starting on the 4th string at the 5th fret. The first note was A. But wait! Your open 3rd string is also A. They must be the same note. Play this A, both on the 4th and the 3rd string as indicated in the figures.

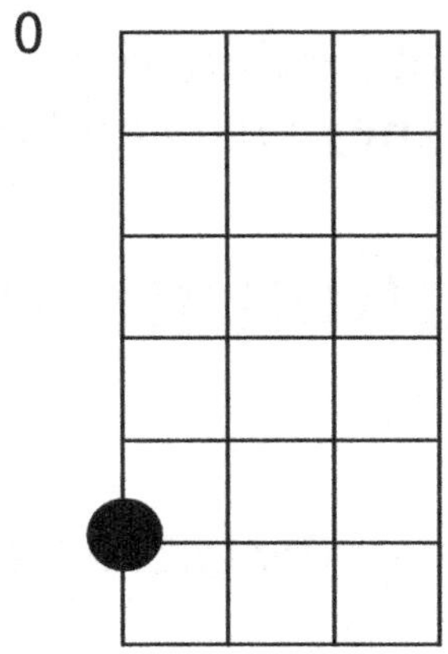

They are the same note!

FIG.63 - 4TH STRING 5TH FRET A

FIG.64 - OPEN 3RD STRING A

At right is a new pattern for the A Major Pentatonic. Right away, you'll notice that it starts on the open 3rd string.

Play it with the fingering indicated, then play the same scale from Figure 62 to confirm they sound the same.

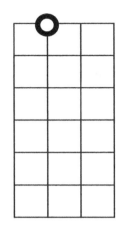

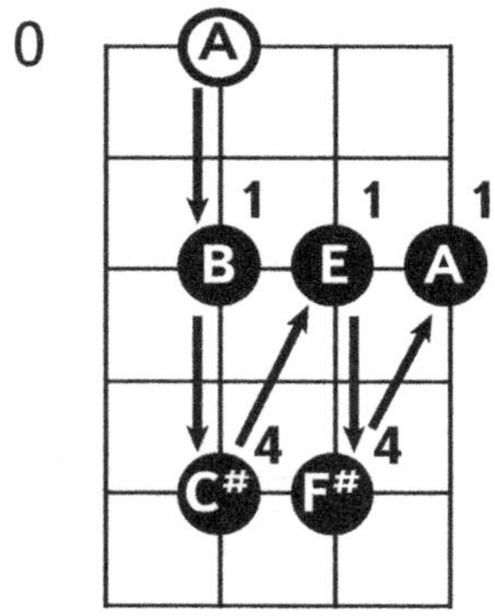

FIG.65 - A MAJOR PENTATONIC

That's pretty cool, right? When making music, it's good to have options of several ways to play a song.

E MAJOR PENTATONIC

Just as you saw how to move the C Major scale to G Major by moving it across the fingerboard, now you'll move the A Major Pentatonic to E Major Pentatonic.

Play the E Major Pentatonic and notice how it uses the same fingering pattern you just used for A Major.

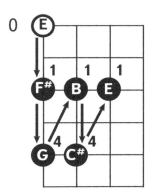

FIG.66 - E MAJOR PENTATONIC

Super! You're getting very flexible, moving scales around the fretboard. Here's another bit of fun: Play E Major Pentatonic an octave higher.

MOVING UP AN OCTAVE

An octave of any note has the same name, but sounds higher in pitch. The two notes together sound so much alike, they're called octaves of each other.

Remembering the pattern you learned for C, G and A Major Pentatonic, play the pattern at right. It is an E Major Pentatonic scale, one octave higher than the one in Figure 66.

Now play the lower E Major Pentatonic from Figure 66. Hear how they sound the same, but in different octaves?

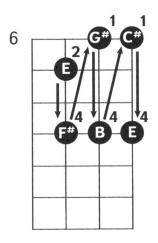

FIG.67 - E MAJOR PENTATONIC

You've already seen quarter-, half- and whole-notes. Here is a combination rhythm that uses both quarter-notes and half-notes. You'll remember a half-note takes the same amount of time as 2 quarter-notes. Out loud, count, "One, Two, Three, Four". Each word is a quarter-note. A half-note would be held for a two-count, like "One, Two" or "Three, Four".

Play these with the Pentatonic scales from Figures 65 and 66.

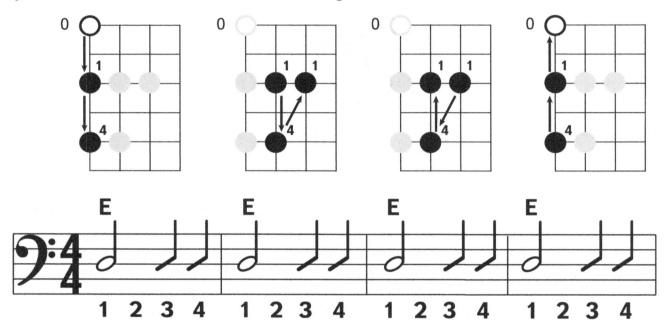

FIG.68 - E MAJOR PENTATONIC MIXED RHYTHM

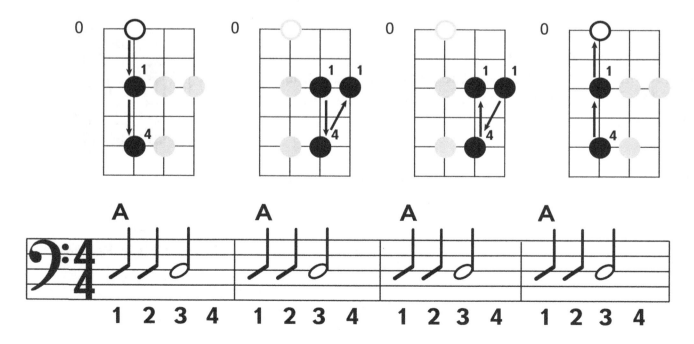

FIG.69 - A MAJOR PENTATONIC MIXED RHYTHM

You know, this is starting to sound a lot like music! Congratulate yourself, musician!

Today's Assignment

Try these bass lines using E and A Major Pentatonic Scales. Notice how in the first exercise, the A Pentatonic starts on the open 3rd string. In the second exercise, it uses a different pattern - one that starts on the 4th string at the 5th fret.

Take time to get these walking bass parts sounding very smooth and even. For now, don't worry about high speed. Slow and steady is the goal here.

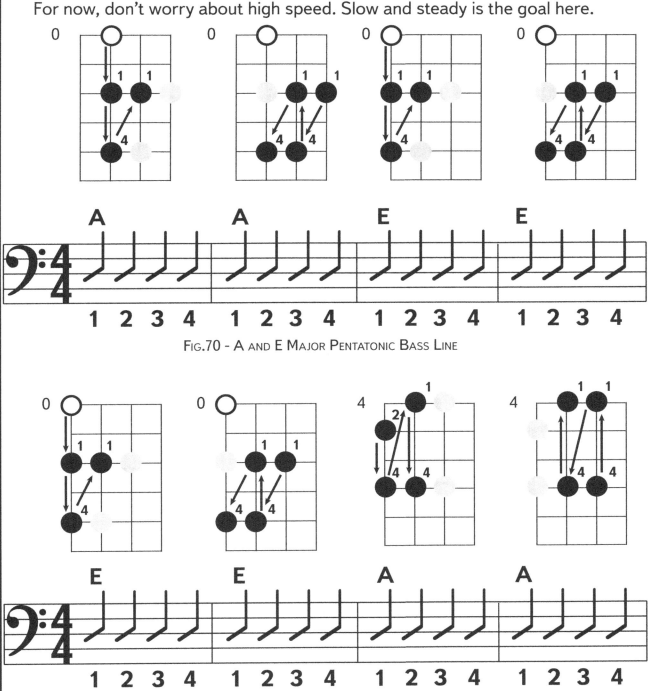

FIG.70 - A AND E MAJOR PENTATONIC BASS LINE

FIG.71 - A AND E MAJOR PENTATONIC BASS LINE

Electric Bass Guitar

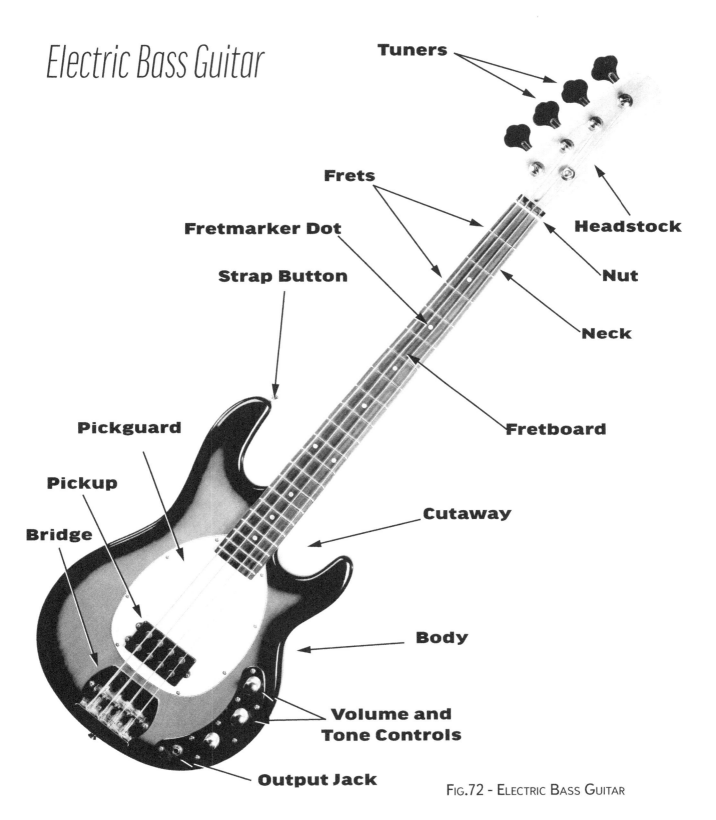

Tuners
Frets
Fretmarker Dot
Strap Button
Headstock
Nut
Neck
Pickguard
Fretboard
Pickup
Cutaway
Bridge
Body
Volume and Tone Controls
Output Jack

FIG.72 - ELECTRIC BASS GUITAR

46 BASS GUITAR BEGINNERS JUMPSTART: A SEEING MUSIC METHOD BOOK

DAY 6 - RIGHT HAND RHYTHMS

Music is made of three elements: melody, harmony and rhythm. Melody is the singable part, generally a single note line. Harmony is all the other notes going on simultaneously that support the melody and develop the chords. Both melodies and harmonies have rhythm, and good rhythm helps keep things interesting.

Bass players use a variety of techniques to create rhythm. Among them are playing with a pick and fingerstyle "walking". Which one you choose will probably depend on your musical tastes and the style you will be playing. Neither is superior, but they both have lots of different uses and are worth knowing. You'll probably prefer one over the other, but spend a little time experimenting with both techniques.

PLAYING WITH A PICK

Pick playing is favored among many rock bassists. Picking produces notes which are strong and clean and stand up well when mixed with loud guitars.

Start by selecting a heavy pick. Picks aren't designated as being for guitar or bass, but lighter picks probably won't work well on heavy bass guitar strings.

LITTLE BITS OF RHYTHM

To prepare for a good rhythm workout, have a look at a new note value: the eighth note.

FIG.73 - EIGHTH-NOTE

As you might expect, there are 8 eighth notes in a measure of 4/4 time. This is one way you could write 8 eighth notes.

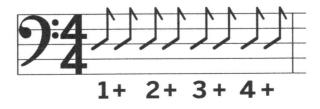

FIG.74 - EIGHTH-NOTES

However, when there are a bunch of eighth notes used together in a measure, it is much more common to see them grouped in twos like this.

Two eighth notes equal one quarter note. The rhythm is counted, "One-and-Two-and-Three-and-Four-and".

FIG.75 - EIGHTH-NOTES

WHAT GOES DOWN MUST COME UP

Picking is made of two parts: the downstroke and the upstroke. Every downstroke must have an upstroke. Otherwise, your picking hand would go down toward the floor and never return, right? The upstroke brings your hand back to its starting position.

Down, up, down, up. That's what we'll work on now, because that motion is the basis for all good rhythm.

Work on this motion silently, at first. Following the down and upstroke symbols, move your picking hand over one string without actually touching it. This is just to get a feel for the motion. Your right hand should be somewhere over the strings and about mid-way between the bridge and the neck. Depending on your bass, you'll probably be right over a pickup.

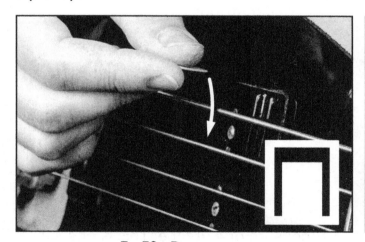

FIG.76 - DOWNSTROKE

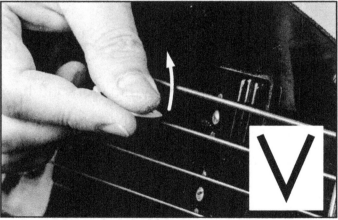

FIG.77 - UPSTROKE

The rhythmic motion you're playing are eighth-notes.

1+ 2+ 3+ 4+

FIG.78 - EIGHTH-NOTES

Now, place your left hand to fret G, 4th string, 3rd fret. Try the same eighth-note strum, pick contacting the string lightly. Down, then up and repeat.

The right amount of contact with the string is very important. Too little contact, you won't make much sound. Too much and the note will sound like a barnyard animal, "BLAAT!" Way too much contact and you might actually break the string. Aim for medium intensity and a full, round sound.

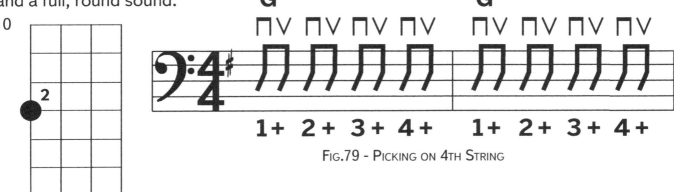

FIG.79 - PICKING ON 4TH STRING

Now, move your fretting hand to C, 3rd string, 3rd fret. Try the same eighth-note strum. Down, then up and repeat.

Your movement shouldn't be any larger than necessary. If your hand swings wildly, you'll have trouble finding speed and accuracy. See how little movement you can give it to still do the job.

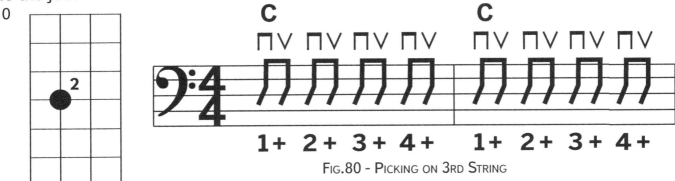

FIG.80 - PICKING ON 3RD STRING

Try the 2nd string, this time moving your fret hand over to F, 2nd string, 3rd fret. Try the downstroke/upstroke strum. Picking on this higher and lighter string feels quite different from picking on the heavy low E string, doesn't it?

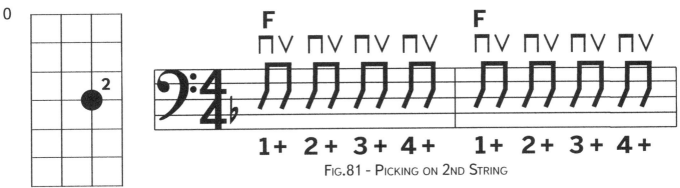

FIG.81 - PICKING ON 2ND STRING

Lastly, move your fretting hand to B flat, 1st string, 3rd fret. Feel how different this is on this thinner string?

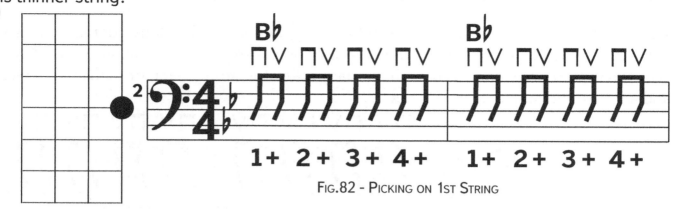

FIG.82 - PICKING ON 1ST STRING

This is the tricky bit about picking on the bass guitar. Different strings require different amounts of picking force and as such, a little different right hand touch. Different notes *feel* different and a good amount of practice is required to play with consistent volume and tone when switching from string to string.

HOW TO ADD UPSTROKES

Here's a basic downstroke pattern. The symbol between notes that kind of looks like the number 7 is an eighth rest. A rest is just a silent note. So, an eighth rest is the length of an eighth note, but silent.

FIG.83 - DOWNSTROKES WITH RESTSTROKES

FIG.84 - EIGHTH-NOTE

If you've been picking the exercises in previous chapters, you may have been only using this pattern until now. Try it again, this time taking note of how often your hand silently makes the upstroke. A silent stroke is called a *reststroke*.

Instead of just four strokes, you were really making eight: four downward and against the strings and four silent upstrokes!

This is a combination of silent and sounded upstrokes. Your picking hand will continue the down, up, down, up steady movement. Just as before, sometimes you'll use silent upstrokes (reststrokes) and sometimes you'll strum the string on the upstrokes.

FIG.85 - COMBINATION OF NOTES AND RESTS

50 BASS GUITAR BEGINNERS JUMPSTART: A SEEING MUSIC METHOD BOOK

Play any string you like, fretted or open. In fact, try the rhythm with several different notes on several strings.

Here's the same strumming pattern, but with quarter notes on beats 2 and 4. It will sound much the same as the previous exercise.

FIG.86 - COMBINATION OF NOTE VALUES

Here is a neat pattern that has some variety.

If you get stuck on any of these rhythms, count them outloud before playing on your bass. The example at right would be counted, "One, Two, Three-and, Four-and".

FIG.87 - COMBINATION OF NOTE VALUES

Sneaky Pro Tip!

If you find playing with the point of the pick difficult or it produces notes with tone that is too bright, try turning the pick and play with its shoulder. The larger and more round corner changes the way picking feels as well as providing a more round tone.

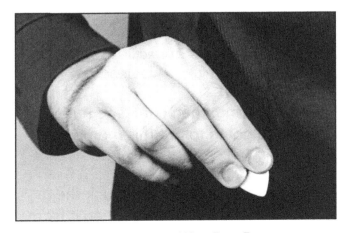

FIG.88 - PLAYING WITH PICK POINT

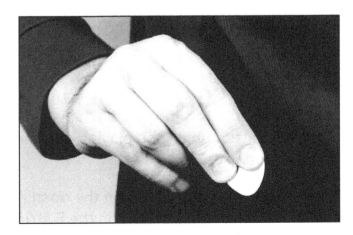

FIG.89 - PLAYING WITH PICK SHOULDER

PLAYING FINGERSTYLE

While using just one finger to pluck every note does work, it's easier to develop speed with two fingers. Alternating between two fingers is a great way to play really fast notes.

To understand the motion you'll be using, extend your right hand pointer finger and middle finger. Now stand your hand up, with those fingers pointing down. If you have a nearby table, make your fingers "walk" across the table, like a miniature person. Your fingers are "walking" like little legs and it's this same alternating motion you'll use on the bass strings.

Fig.90 - "Walking" Fingers

Start by anchoring your right hand thumb against your pickup. Extend your index (pointer) and middle fingers and one at a time, pluck the open low E string with one finger, then the other. Repeat this walking motion. The instant one finger plucks the string, the other should extend, ready to take its turn plucking. Keep going, aiming for smooth, steady notes.

Fig.91 - Index Striking 3rd String, Middle Muting 4th String

Fig.92 - Middle Striking 3rd String, Index Muting 4th String

Notice how with this motion, each finger plucks the low E string, then comes to rest against your thumb. When playing on other strings, you're going to put this moment of rest to good use.

Now try the walking motion on the open A string. This time as your fingers pluck the string, let them come to rest on the E string. They will mute the E string and keep it from accidentally ringing.

52 BASS GUITAR BEGINNERS JUMPSTART: A SEEING MUSIC METHOD BOOK

Keep walking on the A string, fingers alternating. Are the notes from one finger louder than those from the other? If so, make a little adjustment so each finger catches the same amount of string as the other and you'll hear the volume even out. The sound from each finger's pluck should be about the same.

Move on to the open D string. Take it for a walk!

Lastly, give a try on the open G string. Remember that your fingers should come to rest on the next lower string (in this case, the D string).

 # Seeing Sparks! *Quick Tip*

To keep your learning going, here are some subjects you may want to investigate.

Pentatonic Scales
Scale Exercises
Memorizing Your Fretboard
Modal Scale Theory
Complex Time Signatures (5/4, 7/8, etc.)

Today's Assignment

You've been playing combination rhythms using quarter- and eighth-notes. These combinations make music fantastic and much more interesting.

Whether you're using a pick or fingers, start the following chord progressions slowly at first. The goal is very steady rhythm and smooth transitions between chords. Play the root of each chord indicated. For a G Major chord, you'll play G. For C Major, you'll play C, and so on.

If you're picking, follow the up and downstroke symbols. If you're playing fingerstyle, alternate fingers with every note.

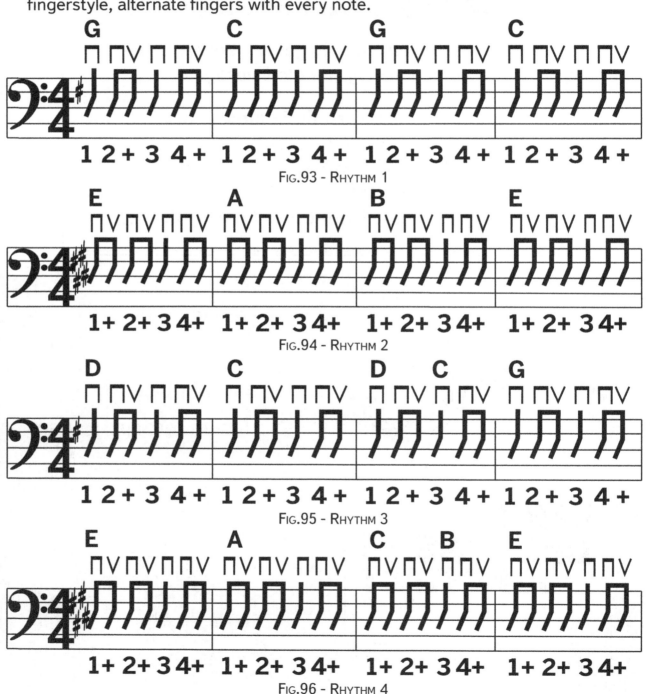

FIG.93 - RHYTHM 1

FIG.94 - RHYTHM 2

FIG.95 - RHYTHM 3

FIG.96 - RHYTHM 4

KNOW YOUR FRETBOARD (PART II)

You've already learned the names of the natural notes up to the 3rd fret. Let's take a look at a very special fret, the 5th fret.

THE 5TH FRET

Remember the first three natural notes on the 4th string? They are E, F and G. Want to guess what the next one is?

It's A and it's found at the 5th fret.

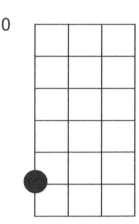

FIG.97 - 4TH STRING 5TH FRET A

What's the name of your 3rd string? It's A as well, right? Well, these are the same note, played two different ways.

Play both these notes to confirm they are the same pitch.

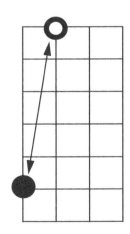

FIG.98 - SAME NOTE ON TWO STRINGS

Sometimes in bass playing, it's really convenient to have a couple of options for a given note. Many notes exist in several places around the neck.

Let's look at some more you already know.

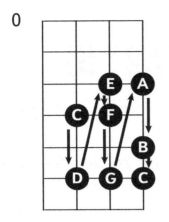

FIG.99 - C MAJOR SCALE

Two of these open string equivalent notes are found in the C Major scale. Start playing the C Major scale. The first note is C. The second note is D. Stop! You're playing the note D on the 3rd string at the 5th fret.

What's the name of the 2nd string? It's D! Confirm they're the same note by playing both the 3rd-string, 5th-fret D and the open 2nd-string D.

Pretty neat, right? Figure 100 shows these open string equivalent notes.

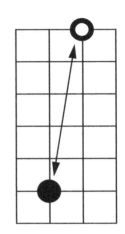

FIG.100 - OPEN STRING EQUIVALENTS

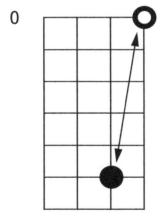

FIG.101 - OPEN STRING EQUIVALENTS

Keep going, you know more than that! Again, let's start playing the C Major scale. C, D, E, F, G..Stop. You should be on the 2nd string at the 5th fret. You've probably already guessed: this G is the same as the open 1st-string G.

Here is a diagram of the equivalent pitches of the open strings: A, D and G.

The fact that there are equivalent notes at the 5th fret is possible because the strings of the bass are tuned the same interval apart. They are all tuned a Perfect 4th apart.

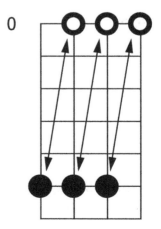

FIG.102 - OPEN STRING EQUIVALENTS

The natural notes of the first three frets can easily be remembered by grouping the 2nd and 3rd strings which share similar fingerings (see chapter "Know Your Fretboard [Part I]").

Many notes on the bass can be found in several places on the fretboard.

The open strings have equivalents at the 5th fret of the lower adjacent string.

Strings are tuned the same interval apart.

Today's Assignment

Review the notes through the 5th fret, starting with the open 4th string, E. Work your way up the natural notes to the 5th fret, saying the names as you go. Take note of the open string equivalents.

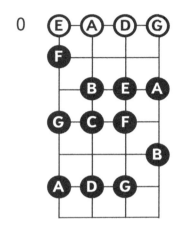

FIG.103 - NATURAL NOTES

58 BASS GUITAR BEGINNERS JUMPSTART: A SEEING MUSIC METHOD BOOK

DAY 7 - THE D MAJOR SCALE

||||||||||||||||||||||||||||||||||||||||||||||||||||||||||||||||||||||||||||

MILESTONE

Play the G Major and C Major scales you now know.

There is a third scale that completes their set as well. It is D Major.

||||||||||||||||||||||||||||||||||||||||||||||||||||||||||||||||||||||||||||

HOW TO PLAY A D MAJOR SCALE

Start with the pattern of the C Major Scale which starts on the 3rd string, 3rd fret. You know that D is the second note of that scale and it is found on the 3rd string at the 5th fret.

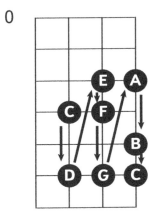

FIG.104 - C MAJOR SCALE

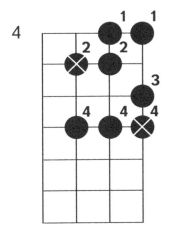

FIG.105 - D MAJOR SCALE

Play this same scale pattern, now starting on D, 3rd string 5th fret.

Since you're already familiar with pentatonic scales, you probably have guessed that the D Major Pentatonic looks very much like the C Major Pentatonic.

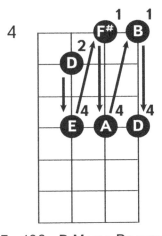

FIG.106 - D MAJOR PENTATONIC

3/4 TIME SIGNATURE

You know that many songs are in 4/4 time. This means there are four quarter-notes per measure. Another time signature is 3/4 (pronounced *three-four*).

3/4 time has three quarter notes per measure. Every waltz is in 3/4 time. That's what makes it a waltz.

3/4 time is counted, "One, Two, Three, One, Two, Three.." Start by just counting a few measures outloud.

Now try this waltz, playing the roots of the chords as indicated. Refer to the chart at right to refresh your memory of the note locations.

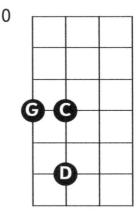

FIG.107 - G, C AND D

FIG.108 - WALTZ IN G MAJOR

Today's Assignment

Here are a variety of mini-songs using G, C and D chords.

Play just the root of each chord using the rhythm indicated. Keep time smoothly and work to make the transitions from chord to chord smooth and seamless.

Many measures use two chords per bar so you'll be changing fingering more frequently. Use a downward motion for each strum.

Figures 111 and 112 are in 3/4 time. Notice how they sound like waltzes!

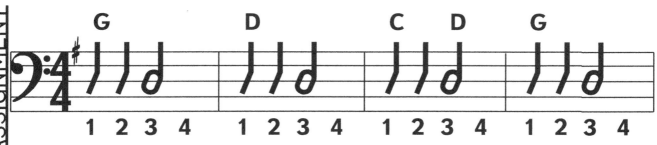

FIG.109 - GDC COMBO RHYTHMS 1

FIG.110 - GDC COMBO RHYTHMS 2

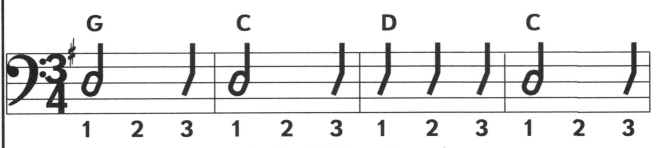

FIG.111 - GDC COMBO RHYTHMS 3

FIG.112 - GDC COMBO RHYTHMS 4

THE D MAJOR SCALE 61

DAY 8 - MINOR SCALES

||||||||||||||||||||||||||||||||||||||||||||||||||||||||||||||||||||||||||||||||

MILESTONE

Play the E Major and A Major scales.

Every scale has a major version and a *minor* version.

||||||||||||||||||||||||||||||||||||||||||||||||||||||||||||||||||||||||||||||||

HOW TO PLAY C MINOR AND G MINOR

FIG.113 - C MINOR NOTE NAMES

Look at the two scales at right. You're familiar with C Major on the left. On the right is the minor version: C minor.

See how there are three notes difference between these scales? E becomes E flat, A becomes A flat and B becomes B flat. Those small changes turn a major scale into a minor scale.

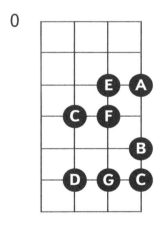

FIG.114 - C MAJOR SCALE

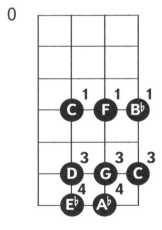

FIG.115 - C MINOR SCALE

Play the C minor version and notice the big difference in sound between it and C Major.

Generally, minor chords are used in songwriting to impart a sad feeling. Major chords, a happy feeling. Isn't it funny how changing just a few notes can do that?

Just as three notes changed, converting C Major to C minor, three notes transform G Major into G minor.

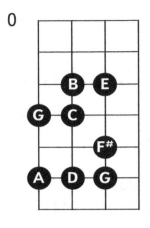

FIG.116 - G MAJOR SCALE

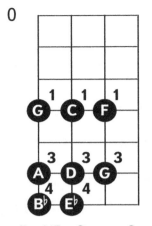

FIG.117 - G MINOR SCALE

HOW TO PLAY A MINOR AND E MINOR

Here are the fretboard diagrams for A and E minor scales. Give each of them a try.

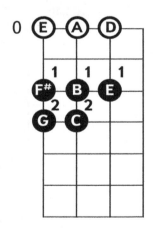

FIG.118 - E MINOR SCALE

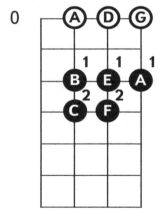

FIG.119 - A MINOR SCALE

All of these scales are called natural minor scales. There are a few varieties of minor scales in the world, but this is the one that gets used most.

HOW TO PLAY MINOR PENTATONICS

You'll recall that pentatonic scales are made of five notes. The major variety uses the root, 2nd, 3rd, 5th and 6th of the major scale. The minor variety is a little different. Have a look.

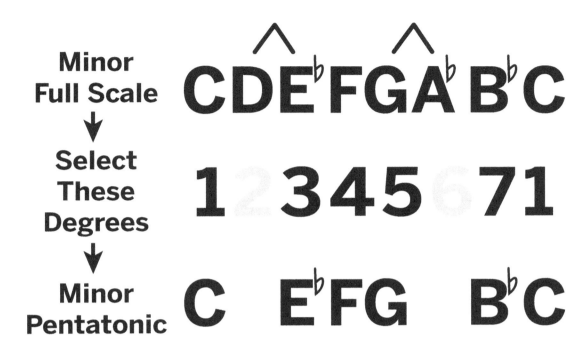

FIG.120 - C MINOR SCALE BECOMING C MINOR PENTATONIC

Play these minor pentatonic scales. Do they sound familiar? Minor pentatonics are what make much of popular music (especially rock or hard rock) possible.

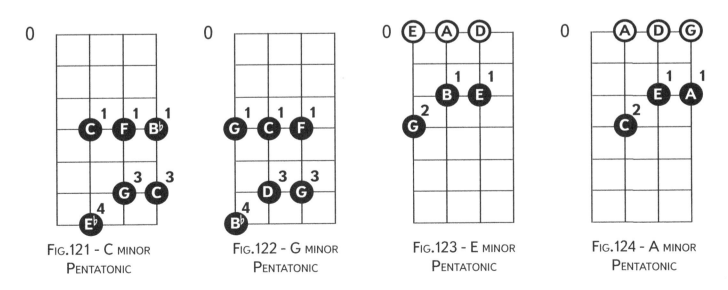

FIG.121 - C MINOR PENTATONIC

FIG.122 - G MINOR PENTATONIC

FIG.123 - E MINOR PENTATONIC

FIG.124 - A MINOR PENTATONIC

PUTTING CHORD FLAVORS TOGETHER

Good music is like good cooking. It's about finding combinations of flavors that are interesting and go together well. Major and minor chords sound great together and create interesting harmonies because of their different flavors.

One chord combination that sounds terrific is C Major and A minor. Another is G Major and E minor. Give these pentatonic combinations a try.

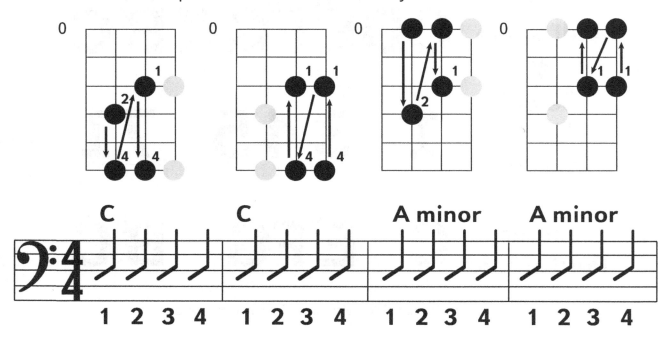

FIG.125 - C MAJOR - A MINOR PROGRESSION

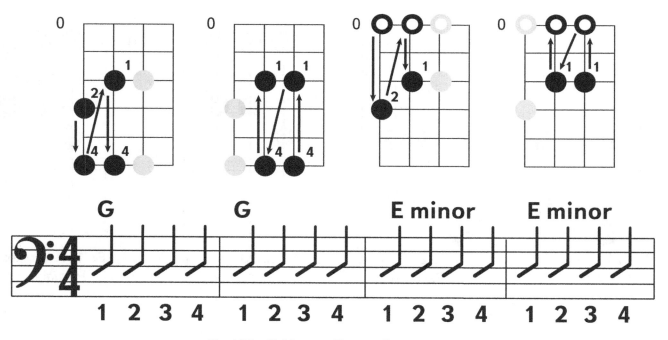

FIG.126 - G MAJOR - E MINOR PROGRESSION

Note: There are many ways to write the chord symbol for the same chord. Here are some of the ways minor chords are indicated.

A min = A⁻ = a

FIG.127 - MINOR KEY NAMING CONVENTIONS

Today's Assignment

Try these progressions of chords, taking note of the different rhythms and time signatures.

Stick to the roots of the chords indicated. This technique, although simple, is a good basic way to begin playing bass lines for any song.

Start the following chord progressions slowly at first. The goal is very steady rhythm and smooth transitions between chords, not high-speed!

FIG.128 - CaGE PROGRESSION

FIG.129 - CaDGCe PROGRESSION

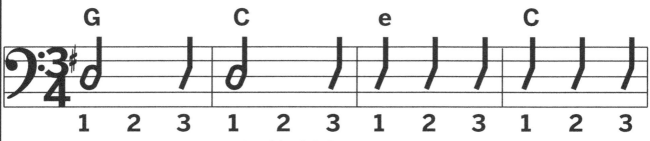

FIG.130 - GCeC PROGRESSION

MINOR SCALES 67

68 BASS GUITAR BEGINNERS JUMPSTART: A SEEING MUSIC METHOD BOOK

DAY 9 - PLAY YOUR FIRST SONGS

IIIIIIIIIIIIIIIIIIIIIIIIIIIIIIIIIIIIIIIIIIIIIIIIIIIIIIIIIIIIIIIIIIIIIIIIIIIIIIIIIIIIIIIIIIII

MILESTONE

Just think of all the scales you've learned in just a few days. Remember all the combinations of note values, rhythms and time signatures you've used.

Time give yourself a pat on the back for assembling all this knowledge in a short amount of time!

IIIIIIIIIIIIIIIIIIIIIIIIIIIIIIIIIIIIIIIIIIIIIIIIIIIIIIIIIIIIIIIIIIIIIIIIIIIIIIIIIIIIIIIIIIII

HOW TO PLAY COUNTRY BASS

Country music originated as dance music. As a bass player, you'll find your job in any kind of dance music is to re-inforce beats 1 and 3 of a measure.

For much of early Country music, the bass line bounced happily between the root of the chord and the 5th of the chord. Remember in the C Major scale, the root is C and the 5th note, or degree, is G. Play this bouncing rhythm as indicated in the fretboard diagrams. Make sure your notes stop cleanly on the quarter note rests.

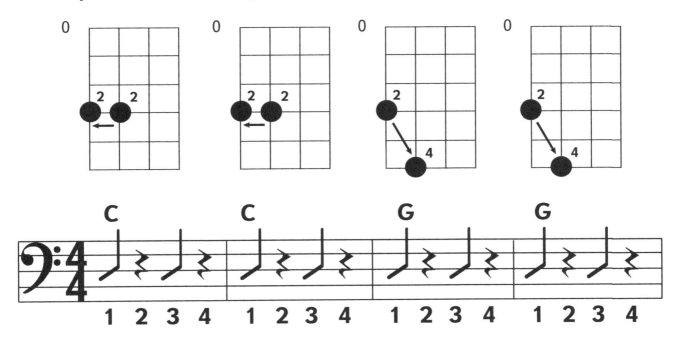

FIG.131 - COUNTRY BASS LINE IN C MAJOR

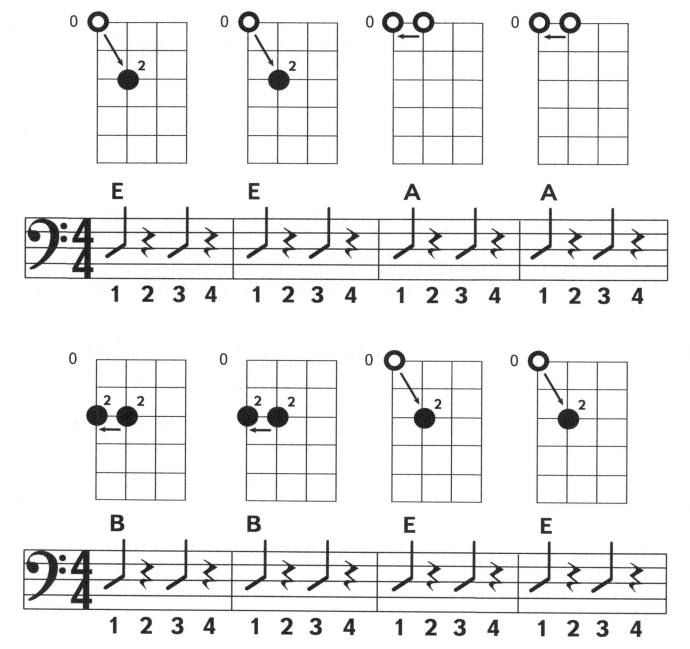

FIG.132 - COUNTRY BASS LINE IN E MAJOR

HOW TO WALK A BLUES BASS LINE

Blues music is recognized and enjoyed everywhere in the world. Perhaps one of the reasons it is so popular is because it has so many varieties.

Additionally, Blues music evolved into Rock and Roll, Country music and much of Jazz. It's certainly a form worth studying!

Blues bass lines often incorporate pentatonic scales. This kind of bass line doesn't sit still! It goes up high and down low which is how it got its name: Walking Bass. It walks all over the place!

Use the patterns in the fretboard diagrams for each indicated chord in the song.

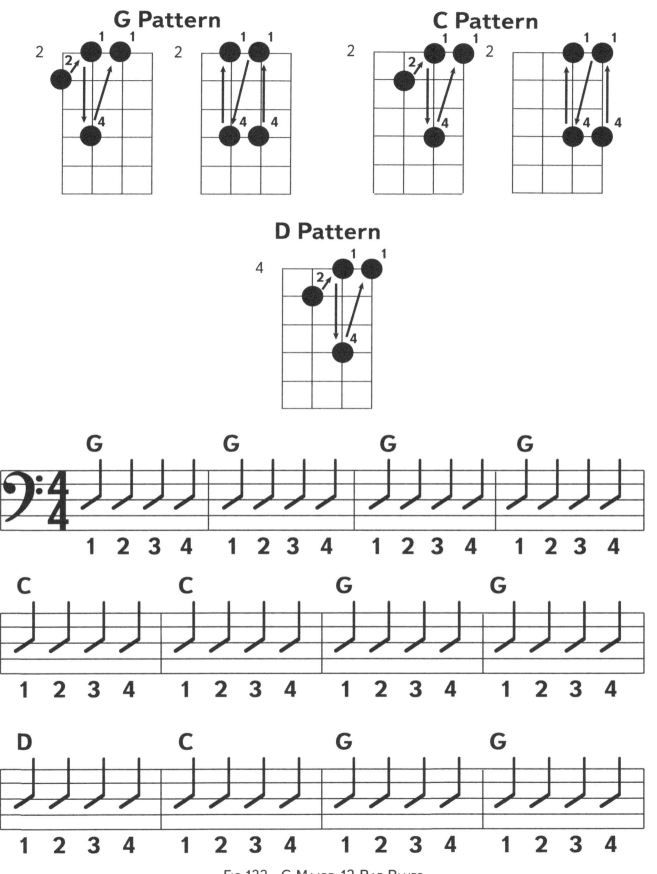

FIG.133 - G MAJOR 12-BAR BLUES

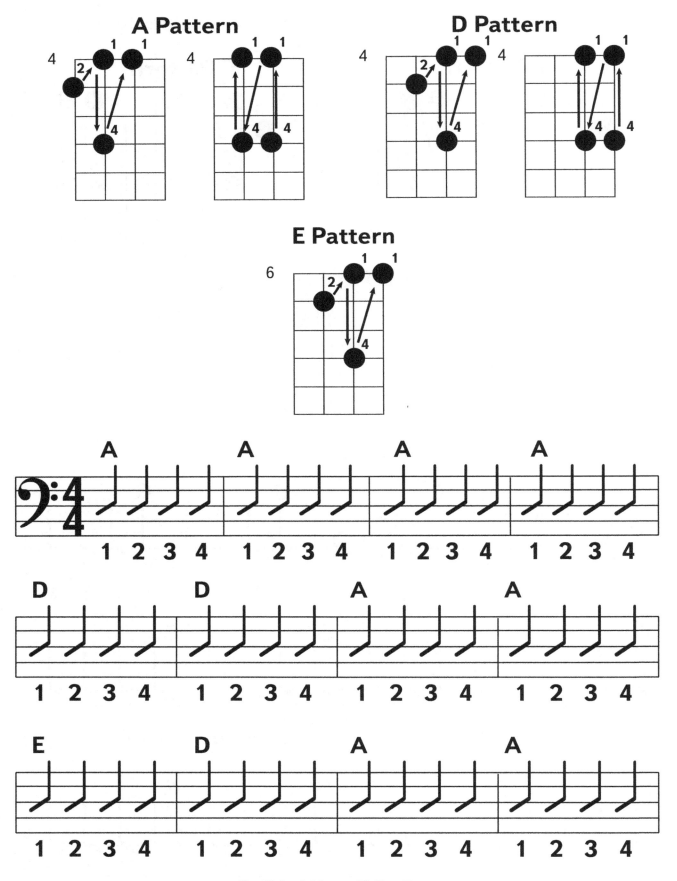

FIG.134 - A MAJOR 12-BAR BLUES

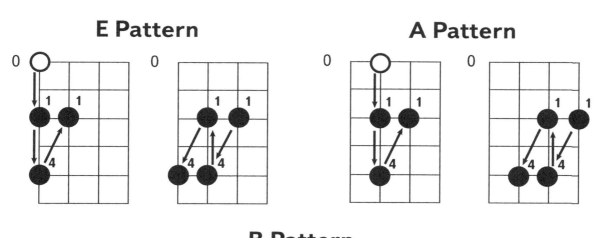

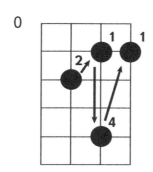

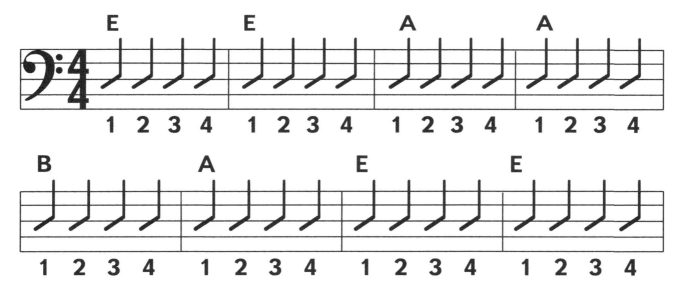

Fig.135 - E Major 8-Bar Blues

HOW TO PLAY A ROCK AND ROLL SONG

Early Rock and Roll took the familiar chord changes of the Blues and started mixing things up. Often the two forms would use the same chords, but Rock and Roll would recombine them, putting a new twist on familiar chords. Energetic rhythms super-charged these songs. Instead of playing each pentatonic note with one quarter note, play them with two eighth notes. The first measure here is played G-G, B-B, D-D, E-E. It's the same progression as the Blues example, but with eighth notes instead of quarter notes.

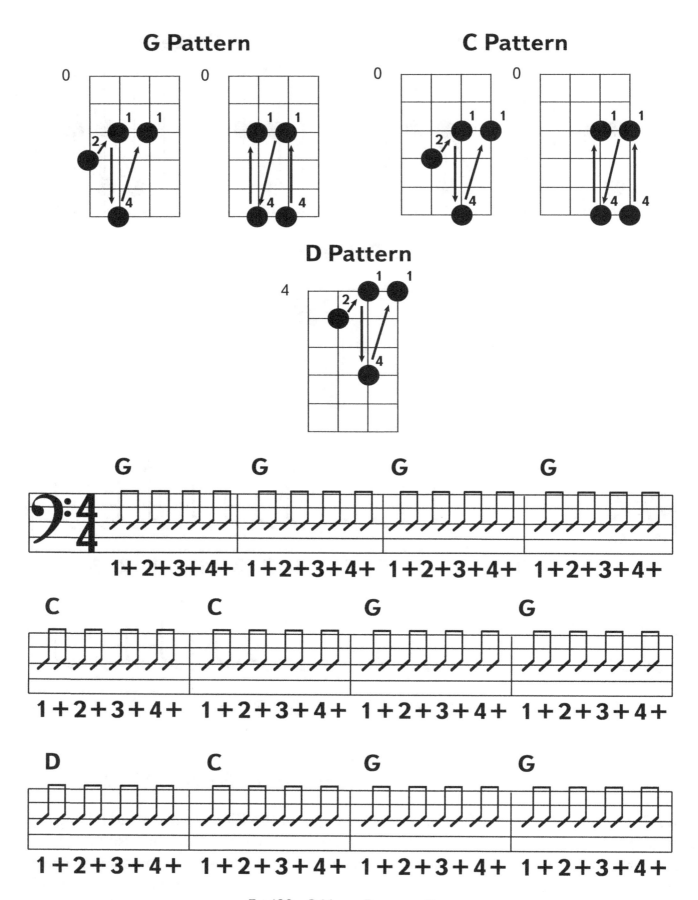

FIG.136 - G MAJOR ROCK AND ROLL

ROCK AND ROLL WITH MINOR CHORDS

Early Rock and Roll music certainly wasn't afraid to experiment! Here's an example of 1950s-style rock using major and minor chords.

This song uses an eighth-note rest followed by an eighth-note, like this:

If you're using a pick, play a reststroke on the eighth-rest followed by an upstroke on the next eighth-note.

Stick to the roots of the chords indicated and watch the rhythm closely! It changes near the end of the song.

Fig.137 - Eighth Rest and Eighth Note

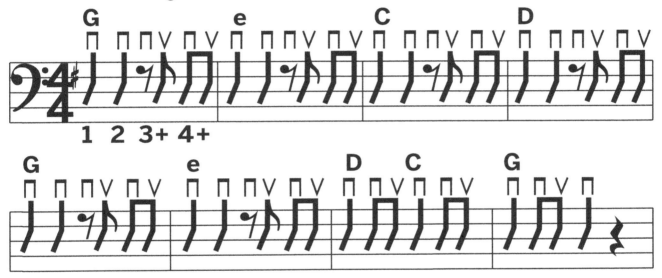

Fig.138 - G Major Rock and Roll

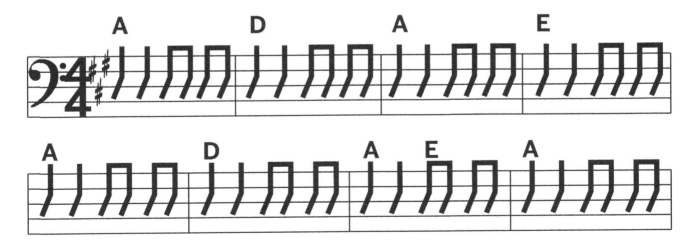

Fig.139 - A Major Rock and Roll

Today's Assignment

Continue practicing the songs in this chapter. Then, continue reading the next chapter where you'll learn more about creating your own songs with combinations of chords and rhythms you like. Of course, you may not like every combination of chords you try. That's normal. Write down the chord combinations and rhythms you find interesting on the sheet music at the end of this book.

DAY 10 - CREATING NEW BASS LINES

|||||||||||||||||||||||||||||||||||||||||||||||||||||||||||||||||||||||||||||

MILESTONE

You learned many scales, rhythms and patterns on the bass. So, now how do you choose from all these options?

As a bass player, how should you approach your part in a song?

|||||||||||||||||||||||||||||||||||||||||||||||||||||||||||||||||||||||||||||

Bass players have a fundamental role in the construction of music. The bass generally isn't the lead instrument, such as a voice or guitar solo. The bass is usually the only instrument on stage that is both keeping solid time (defining the beat) throughout the song as well as defining the chords that are passing. Think about it: Drums don't really have pitches that change, all the other instruments may drop out from time to time. It's the job of the bass player to hold the rhythm together while supporting the chord structure. Wow, that's a really important job!

With that in mind, look at some of the guideposts you'll use to make music.

CHORDS AND SCALES GO TOGETHER

It probably isn't surprising to hear that a major scale sounds good when played over a major chord. You already know that a major pentatonic goes with a major chord, a minor pentatonic with a minor chord. There is a really great reason for this. Those chords that guitar players and keyboard players play come from scales. Chords are derived from scales and the bass guitar is great at playing various scales which help reinforce the chords the rest of the instruments are playing.

CHORDS COME FROM SCALES

The basis for all major and minor chords are just three notes: the root, 3rd and 5th degrees of their scale. For example, from the C Major Scale (C, D, E, F, G, A, B, C), select the 1st, 3rd and 5th notes: C, E and G. C Major chords are built of these 3 notes.

Think about this for a minute. If guitar players have 6 strings and strum them all, how can they be playing just 3 notes?

Sometimes instrumentalists will reinforce a chord by playing the root, 3rd and 5th as well as *octaves* of those notes. That's how a guitar player can strum a chord on all 6 strings at the same time. They play the root, 3rd and 5th, as well as octaves of some or all of those notes. Only 3 notes are necessary, but doubling those with octaves sounds more full.

Bassists rarely play more than one note simultaneously simply because in the low registers, multiple notes can get muddy very quickly. Instead, the bass player plays the song's chords *one note at a time*.

This is a pretty heavy idea. Bass players, in a real sense, are playing chords one note at a time rather than several notes simultaneously. What a cool way to support a song!

Here's your job: Create bass lines that frequently use the root, 3rd and 5th of the chord's scale. Remember the major pentatonic? What scale tones does it use? Root, 2nd, 3rd, 5th, 6th. Hey! The root, 3rd and 5th are in there!

> *Instead of playing chord notes simultaneously, the bass player plays the song's chords <u>one note at a time</u>.*

Remember the minor pentatonic? What scale tones does it use? Root, 3rd, 4th, 5th, 7th. Eureka! It also uses the root, 3rd and 5th!

No wonder pentatonic scales make great bass lines! They come loaded with really important notes.

You should know that some chords include more notes than just the root, 3rd and 5th to add more color to the sound. For now, just remember that the most important thing you can do in the bass register is play the root. It should be in almost every measure you ever play. Also try to work in the 3rd and 5th if you can. And if you want to do some walking around, pentatonic scales are a great tool.

DEVELOP YOUR STRATEGIES

You've already seen many examples of various rhythms and patterns which hold a big variety of bass lines: Country 1-5 bouncing, Blues Walking Bass, Rock and Roll eighth notes and just good old simple quarter notes on the root of the chord. These are various approaches to defining the rhythm or pulse of the song. No doubt, you'll learn many more ways to compose a bass line and you'll want to keep all of these ideas around. They're like strategies you can use to fill out your part and keep things interesting.

ASSIGNMENT

Today's Assignment

Revisit the bass lines you've learned throughout this book and examine the note choices. Can you spot the root, 3rd and 5th in many of those lines?

Now try creating your own bass lines with combinations of chords, scales and rhythms you like. Are you ready? Of course you are!

Of course, you may not like every combination of notes or chords you try. That's normal. Write down the chord combinations, bass lines and rhythms you find interesting on the sheet music at the end of this book.

 Seeing Sparks *Quick Tip*

You're now learning the fundamentals of music theory. Music theory is a set of guidelines that make music's elements go together well and sound great.

The time you spend learning the fundamentals will pay off in a big, big way as you make music in the future. If you know theory, you'll never be left wondering what to play.

Join our "Seeing Sparks" newsletter to get more quick tips and recommendations for playing.
Sign up for free at seeingmusicbooks.com!

80 BASS GUITAR BEGINNERS JUMPSTART: A SEEING MUSIC METHOD BOOK

MILESTONES IN MUSIC

Time to congratulate yourself on all you've learned!

- How to read fretboard diagrams

- Note names through the first 5 frets

- Time signatures and note values (eighth, quarter, half and whole)

- Major and minor scales

- Many commonly used rhythms

- Picking and fingerstyle techniques

- C Major and G Major scales

- Major and minor pentatonic scales

- Country, Blues and Rock and Roll Songs

- How to create new bass lines using various strategies

Today's Assignment

Keep learning! You're well on your way to total bass guitar and musical knowledge! Explore the vast world of music and dive into everything you find interesting. You already have to tools to make music and begin answering the questions you'll discover along the way.

There are several books in the *Seeing Music* family you may find interesting to develop your knowledge and skill. *Seeing Music* books put you inside the mind of professional guitarists everywhere who organize their vast knowledge by very simple visual means. Our books give you the tools to continue teaching yourself, to be able to play anything, anytime.

Keep on makin' music, musician!

SCALE AND NOTE REFERENCE

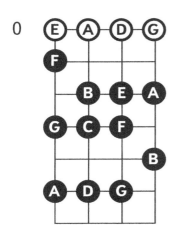

Fig.140 - Natural Notes

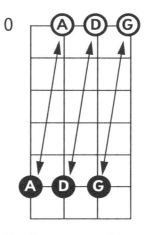

Fig.141 - Open-string Equivalents

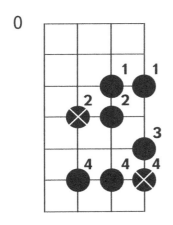

Fig.142 - C Major Scale

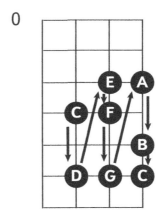

Fig.143 - C Major Scale

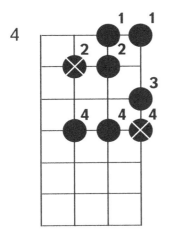

Fig.144 - D Major Scale

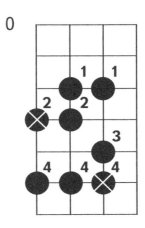

Fig.145 - G Major Scale

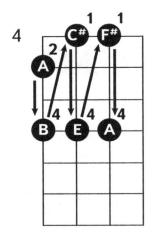

FIG.146 - A MAJOR PENTATONIC

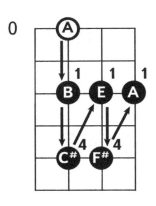

FIG.147 - A MAJOR PENTATONIC

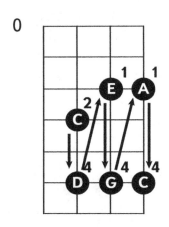

FIG.148 - C MAJOR PENTATONIC

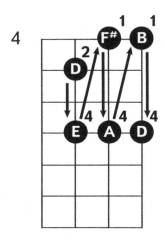

FIG.149 - D MAJOR PENTATONIC

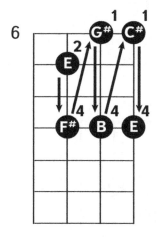

FIG.150 - E MAJOR
PENTATONIC

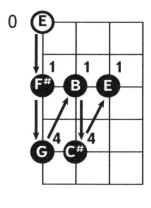

FIG.151 - E MAJOR
PENTATONIC

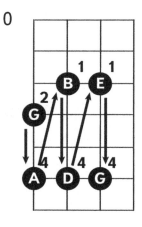

FIG.152 - G MAJOR
PENTATONIC

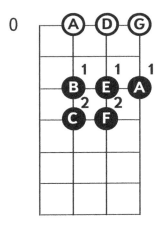

FIG.153 - A MINOR SCALE

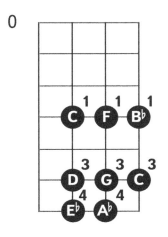

FIG.154 - C MINOR SCALE

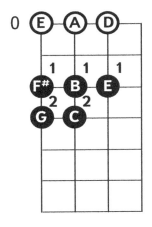

FIG.155 - E MINOR SCALE

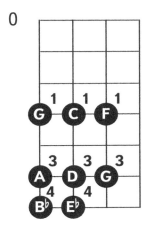

FIG.156 - G MINOR SCALE

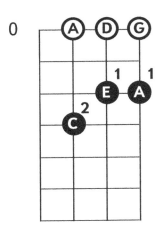

FIG.157 - A MINOR
PENTATONIC

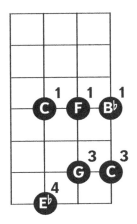

FIG.158 - C MINOR
PENTATONIC

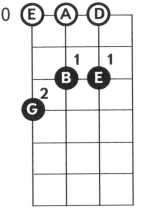

FIG.159 - E MINOR
PENTATONIC

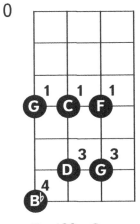

FIG.160 - G MINOR
PENTATONIC

BLANK DIAGRAMS AND STAFF PAPER

Fretboard Diagrams

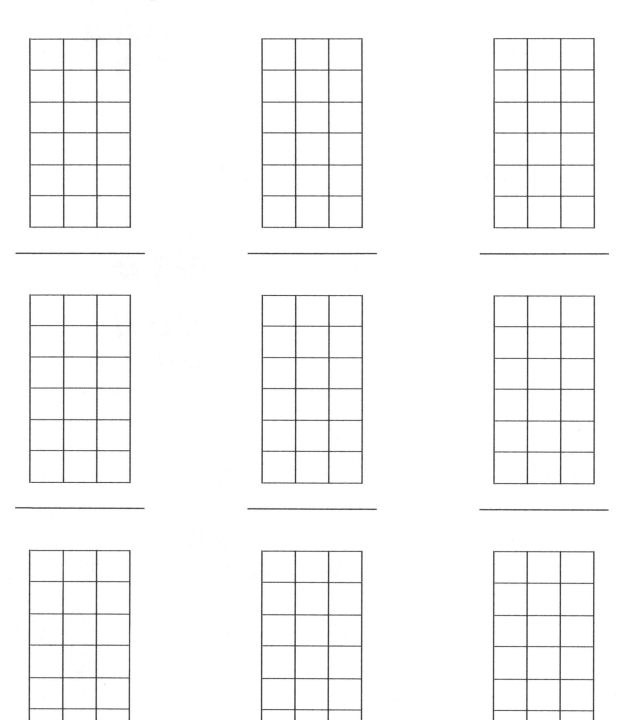

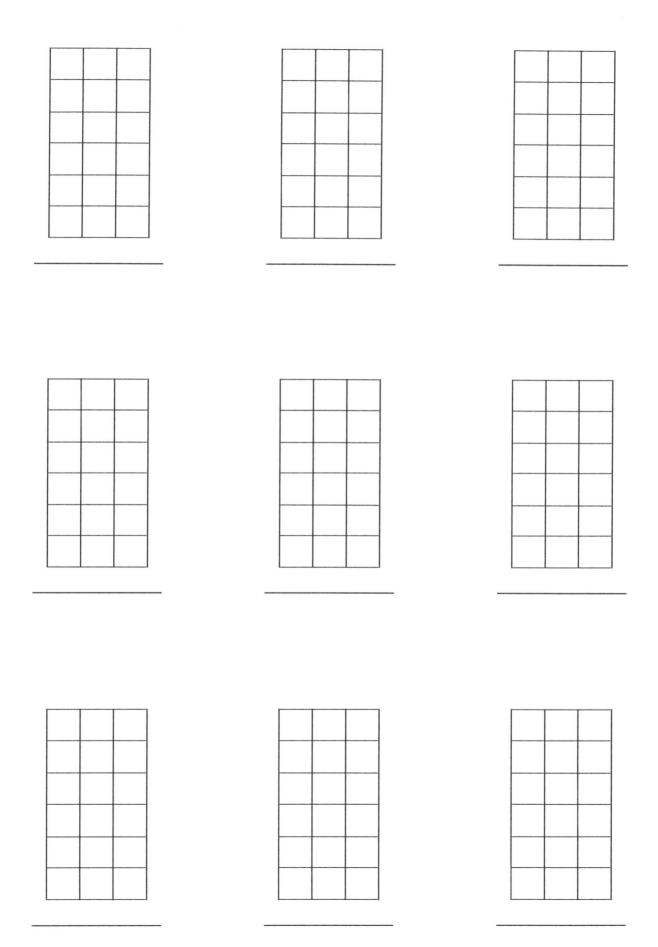

BASS GUITAR BEGINNERS JUMPSTART: A SEEING MUSIC METHOD BOOK

Staff Paper

SEEING MUSIC
METHOD BOOKS

90 BASS GUITAR BEGINNERS JUMPSTART: A SEEING MUSIC METHOD BOOK

Made in the USA
Las Vegas, NV
29 November 2023